T0121843

THE
TRUTH
OF THE
MATTER

THE
TRUTH
OF THE
MATTER

**A Biblical Evaluation of Many of the Confusing
Bible Doctrines Afloat Today**

WILLIAM L. LAUGHLIN

iUniverse, Inc.
Bloomington

The Truth of the Matter
A Biblical Evaluation of Many of the Confusing Bible Doctrines Afloat Today

Copyright © 2010, 2013 by William L. Laughlin.

All rights reserved. No part of this book may be used or reproduced by any means, graphic, electronic, or mechanical, including photocopying, recording, taping or by any information storage retrieval system without the written permission of the publisher except in the case of brief quotations embodied in critical articles and reviews.

iUniverse books may be ordered through booksellers or by contacting:

iUniverse
1663 Liberty Drive
Bloomington, IN 47403
www.iuniverse.com
1-800-Authors (1-800-288-4677)

Because of the dynamic nature of the Internet, any web addresses or links contained in this book may have changed since publication and may no longer be valid. The views expressed in this work are solely those of the author and do not necessarily reflect the views of the publisher, and the publisher hereby disclaims any responsibility for them.

Any people depicted in stock imagery provided by Thinkstock are models, and such images are being used for illustrative purposes only.
Certain stock imagery © Thinkstock.

ISBN: 978-1-4759-7642-7 (sc)
ISBN: 978-1-4759-7644-1 (hc)
ISBN: 978-1-4759-7643-4 (ebk)

Printed in the United States of America

iUniverse rev. date: 02/28/2013

Except as noted when used, all scripture is from the Authorized or King James Version.

CONTENTS

Introduction...vii

INTRODUCTION

Never before in the Christian dispensation have so many been so confused over so many different doctrines preached by so many different religious organizations. The apostle Paul warned us about such confusion. Even the mainline fundamental denominations are buying into popular doctrines of the end times. We need to remember that Satan is working overtime in these last days because he knows he has only a short time before final judgment.

Listen to the apostle Paul in 1 Corinthians 14:26: "How is it then, brethren? when ye come together, every one of you hath a psalm, hath a doctrine, hath a tongue, hath a revelation, hath an interpretation. Let all things be done unto edifying."

The purpose of this book is to examine some of the more prominent of these doctrines in the light of God's Word. Man is morally responsible to God and will meet God and the Word of God at the judgment on the last day. At that day, the books will be opened and man will be judged according to what is written in the books. The books are the Word of God, the Bible, and the book of life, God's registry of the redeemed. Life is too short and eternity is too long to be in error concerning God's desire and purpose for us.

How can a religious world know the truth and the peace of God when there is so much controversy and disagreement from preacher to preacher? Whom can you believe? How can you know the truth? There is only one way any soul can come to knowledge of the truth, and that is to seek the truth. To come to knowledge of the truth we must know where to find the truth. Worshipping God in spirit and in truth is mandatory.

John 4:23-24 says, "But the hour cometh, and now is, when the true worshippers shall worship the Father in spirit and in truth: for the Father seeketh such to worship him. God is a Spirit: and they that worship him must worship him in spirit and in truth."

Jesus promised that we would know the truth.

John 8:32 says, "And ye shall know the truth, and the truth shall make you free."

The world, the antireligious, and the unbelievers cannot know the truth because the truth is a spirit that must be received into the heart of the believer.

John 14:17 says, "Even the Spirit of truth; whom the world cannot receive, because it seeth him not, neither knoweth him: but ye know him; for he dwelleth with you, and shall be in you."

And John 16:13 says, "Howbeit when he, the Spirit of truth, is come, he will guide you into all truth: for he shall not speak of himself; but whatsoever he shall hear, that shall he speak: and he will shew you things to come."

The truth is the *Word of God*. It is the Word and the Spirit of truth, which is the Holy Spirit that sanctifies the Christian heart.

"Sanctify them through thy truth: thy word is truth" (John 17:17).

"For the hope which is laid up for you in heaven, whereof ye heard before in the word of the truth of the gospel" (Colossians 1:5).

"Study to shew thyself approved unto God, a workman that needeth not to be ashamed, rightly dividing the word of truth" (2 Timothy 2:15).

To truly identify the Word of truth, all we need is to read St. John 1:1, which says that Jesus Christ is the Word. Jesus also said that He was the "way, the *truth* and the life." In this scripture, we see that in the beginning was "the Word," the Word was "with God," and the Word "was God."

John 1:1 says, "In the beginning was the Word, and the Word was with God, and the Word was God."

Therefore, Jesus is the "Word" of God; the gospel is the declaration of that "Word." The Old and New Testaments of the Bible make up the "Word of God," and the Bible is the only authoritative source that will validate or invalidate any doctrine put forth by any man or organization. Any attempt to alter, eliminate, or add to the truth contained in the scriptures will face the wrath of Almighty God.

Revelation 22:18-19 says, "For I testify unto every man that heareth the words of the prophecy of this book, If any man shall add unto these things, God shall add unto him the plagues that are written in this book: And if any man shall take away from the words of the book of this prophecy, God shall take away his part out of the book of life, and out of the holy city, and from the things which are written in this book."

Based on the above, we will use the Bible as the authority to prove or disprove any doctrine addressed in this book. Other references used will be only as a support to the Bible; in no way will they be used to promote any doctrine not addressed in the Bible.

CHAPTER ONE

Justification

Justification is a term used to describe a spiritual condition of the heart when one believes on the shed blood of Jesus Christ for the remission of sins. Other terms are *born again* and *saved.* We are "saved from our sins." We are "justified" before God because of the transforming grace of the Lord Jesus Christ.

Biblical references to justification can be found in the following passages:

> "And the publican, standing afar off, would not lift up so much as his eyes unto heaven, but smote upon his breast, saying, God be merciful to me a sinner. I tell you, this man went down to his house justified rather than the other: for every one that exalteth himself shall be abased; and he that humbleth himself shall be exalted" (Luke 18:13-14).

> "For not the hearers of the law are just before God, but the doers of the law shall be justified" (Romans 2:13).

> "Therefore by the deeds of the law there shall no flesh be justified in his sight: for by the law is the knowledge of sin" (Romans 3:20).

> "Being justified freely by his grace through the redemption that is in Christ Jesus" (Romans 3:20).

We can see by the above scriptures that justification is the transforming work of the redeeming grace of the Lord Jesus Christ. No man is justified by the "works of the law." In the scripture referenced above, the "works of the law" relate to the Old Testament rules, regulations, rites, and ordinances. In the New Testament dispensation, the "works of the law" would be regulations, procedures, and rituals imposed on people by men and organizations. Some religious bodies will admit members who agree to honor the tenets of the organization and support it with attendance and money. Others will admit members who follow some procedure or ritual. Some require a contract, and others demand a course of education. All such requirements are things the applicant can do. I can sign a contract. I can submit to baptism. I can attend an indoctrination course. I can support with attendance and money. There is no miracle in any of the aforementioned "works," and they therefore are not in any sense related to the experience of justification. There is nothing we can "do" to be "saved."

Being "saved" or "born again" is a divine work wrought in the heart by God through the exercising of faith in the cleansing blood of Jesus Christ. It is a renewing, a transformation, and a re-creation of the human heart with the purpose of restoring it to the condition intended by God in the creation of the human race. God created man in "His own image," holy, sinless, eternal, and much more. God endowed Adam with His own attributes. When Adam sinned, he gave up the godly attributes and took on himself carnal or sinful attributes. God, not being willing for man to perish without hope, prepared the means for man's restoration to the "image of God." The plan of God was to first, remove the sin and second, reintroduce His Spirit into the human heart. Jesus established the first step by taking the guilt of man's committed sins on Himself and dying on the cross with them and thereby rendering the believer guiltless, since his sins died on the cross with Christ. The believer is now justified by his faith in the cleansing blood of Jesus Christ. The second part will be treated in the section on sanctification.

First Peter 1:18-19 says, "Forasmuch as ye know that ye were not redeemed with corruptible things, as silver and gold, from your vain conversation received by tradition from your fathers; But with the precious blood of Christ, as of a lamb without blemish and without spot."

Jesus is identified as the "lamb of God." We need to understand that sin is the reason Adam lost his salvation in the beginning. We are also told that because of that sin, all mankind take on the attributes of their father, Adam, with his sinful and carnal nature. "For all have sinned and come short of the glory of God" (Romans 3:23).

No man can deny his guilt. These hands did the deed. This eye looked and this mind dwelled on the lust. No honest man can say, "I have never sinned." Consequently, we all need God's intervention for our justification before Him. Since the Word of God declares that "all have sinned" and that the "wages of sin is death" (Romans 6:23), we comprehend that man is under the judgment of death. God has declared that "the soul that sinneth, it shall die," according to Ezekiel 18:4. Consequently, all men are under the judgment and penalty of death for sin.

Since this judgment is the judgment of God and the Word of God is immutable, God has no choice but to execute His judgments against the sinner: "The soul that sinneth, it shall die." The only way that God's Word can be honored is for the sinner to die. There is no other option. By God's love and mercy, God sent Jesus to be the propitiation for the sins of mankind.

First John 4:10 says, "Herein is love, not that we loved God, but that he loved us, and sent his Son to be the propitiation for our sins."

Romans 3:25 says, "Whom God hath set forth to be a propitiation through faith in his blood, to declare his righteousness for the remission of sins that are past, through the forbearance of God."

God in His great love for us gave us a substitute, the "lamb of God," to take our punishment to Himself and suffer the penalty imposed by God the Father. Remember that the penalty for sin is death. Jesus became our advocate and intermediary between our sins and the judgment of God. Also remember that it is God's plan to inflict the penalty of man's sin on His son Jesus that we might be set free.

According to 2 Corinthians 5:21, "For he hath made him to be sin for us, who knew no sin; that we might be made the righteousness of God in him."

First Peter 2:24 says, "Who his own self bare our sins in his own body on the tree that we, being dead to sins, should live unto righteousness: by whose stripes ye were healed."

Justification is the heart-transforming power of our heavenly Father through the sacrificial death of the Lord Jesus Christ. When Jesus by God's command accepted our guilt, God according to His own commandment sent Jesus to the cross to pay the price for sins. Jesus was our sacrifice. He became guilty in our place and died the death we should have suffered ourselves. But, because of Jesus shedding His blood in our behalf, we can stand before God with sins forgiven. Our sins are not only forgiven but actually destroyed by death on the cross. Our sins are removed from us as far as the east is from the west. They are cast into the depths of the sea. We are free. We are justified.

CHAPTER TWO

Sanctification

As we saw in the section on justification, sanctification is a state of grace. Most of our mainline churches still teach on the subject of sanctification, but their understanding of it has deteriorated. Reaching back into history, the Bible and most of its soul-saving doctrines were lost during the Dark Ages when the common man could not get a copy of the scriptures. For several centuries it was even a crime for the common man to possess a copy of the Bible. The clergy declared the doctrine as they wanted and religion became just that, "religion" and not spiritual life. A priest during the first centuries of the Christian era was quoted as saying, "We used to believe that salvation was an inner experience, but now we have found it to be only an outward expression." Thus, during the Dark Ages, AD 530 to AD 1530, only a precious few knew the saving grace and the masses of religious people had only "religion." It was in the sixteenth century when Martin Luther, a Catholic monk, saw the truth that "the just shall live by faith" and started preaching "justification," the saving grace of the Lord Jesus Christ through believing on His death and resurrection. Thus, the Protestant Reformation was born. In the eighteenth century, God enlightened many churchmen on the doctrine of sanctification. Prominently, we see men like John and Charles Wesley, Dwight L. Moody, and others who learned that justification was only half of the plan of salvation and that a second grace was needed to empower us for effective service. With the foregoing as our foundation, let us proceed into the study of Bible sanctification.

A Second Work of Grace

Because many of our modern ministries have lost the experience, they no longer teach it as a second work of grace, but as a grace received with and as a part of justification. The Bible very clearly teaches that sanctification is a definite "second" work of grace to be sought and received subsequent to justification. I think we all can agree that Jesus considered His disciples saved.

John 13:10 says, "Jesus saith to him, He that is washed needeth not save to wash his feet, but is clean every whit: and ye are clean, but not all."

At this meeting with the disciples for the Last Supper, Jesus declared that except for Judas, they were all clean spiritually.

John 17:14-17 says, "I have given them thy word; and the world hath hated them, because they are not of the world, even as I am not of the world. I pray not that thou shouldest take them out of the world, but that thou shouldest keep them from the evil. They are not of the world, even as I am not of the world. Sanctify them through thy truth: thy word is truth."

In the above scripture, Jesus in his prayer to the Father marks His disciples as being "not of the world." If they were not of the world, what were they of? They were "in Christ" and as such had entered the "kingdom of heaven." Jesus Himself told His disciples in Luke 17:21 that the kingdom of God was "within" them: "Neither shall they say, Lo here! or, lo there! for, behold, the kingdom of God is within you."

The prophet Ezekiel, speaking for God, says that the Spirit of God will be placed within His followers: "And I will put my spirit within you, and cause you to walk in my statutes, and ye shall keep my judgments, and do them" (Ezekiel 36:27).

In His final instructions before His ascension, Jesus told His disciples that they should not attempt to enter their ministerial service yet, but that they should wait in Jerusalem until they had been endued with power from on high. The power referenced by Jesus was the promise of God by Ezekiel to put His spirit within them. Thus Jesus used the term *endued*. Since Jesus says "I send" the promise, it is apparent that the promise had not yet been received at the time of his departure.

"And, behold, I send the promise of my Father upon you: but tarry ye in the city of Jerusalem, until ye be endued with power from on high" (Luke 24:49).

Jesus also declared in John 16:7 that the promise would not come while He was still in the flesh, but that He would "send" it after He had departed: "Nevertheless I tell you the truth; it is expedient for you that I go away: for if I go not away, the Comforter will not come unto you; but if I depart, I will send him unto you."

Jesus also lets us know that the promise of the Spirit cannot be received by the unregenerate. The world has no claim on the blessings of God, but only believers can receive the promise.

John 14:17 says, "Even the Spirit of truth; whom *the world cannot receive*, because it seeth him not, neither knoweth him: but ye know him; for he dwelleth with you, and shall be in you."

As we can see in the preceding scripture, the world or the unsaved cannot receive the Spirit. Jesus had declared that the Spirit was "with" them, meaning Himself, and should be "in them," meaning the Holy Spirit. And, Jesus said that "after" His departure, the Spirit would be sent into their hearts. Jesus' resurrection was followed only a few days later by Pentecost and the infilling of the disciples with the Holy Ghost.

Acts 2:1-4 says, "And when the day of Pentecost was fully come, they were all with one accord in one place. And suddenly there came a sound from heaven as of a rushing mighty wind, and it filled all the house where they were sitting. And there appeared unto them cloven tongues like as of fire, and it sat upon each of them. And they were all filled with the Holy Ghost, and began to speak with other tongues, as the Spirit gave them utterance."

These disciples, whom Jesus had declared to be clean, had been filled with the Spirit of God as promised by God through Ezekiel. They also were endued with power as they began to speak among the people of Jerusalem in the languages of the various people. We also see Peter, who only days before was terrified to confess Christ, now boldly standing before those who were guilty of condemning Christ to death, pointing his finger at these evildoers and declaring that "with wicked hands" they were guilty of His blood.

Acts 2:22-23 says, "Ye men of Israel, hear these words; Jesus of Nazareth, a man approved of God among you by miracles and wonders and signs, which God did by him in the midst of you, as ye yourselves also know: Him, being delivered by the determinate counsel and foreknowledge of God, ye have taken, and by wicked hands have crucified and slain."

Note the difference between the "unfilled" Peter terrified to confess Christ at His trial and the "filled" Peter who now boldly stands before the same people, exposing their guilt with such power that they cry out "Men and brethren, what must we do." This is the "power from on high" that Jesus commanded they wait for. Without this power, they would be as weak as Peter had been and thus ineffective in their ministry. We see further proof that sanctification is a second work of grace as the apostle Paul discovers "unsanctified" people in his missionary journeys.

Acts 19:2-3 says, "He said unto them, Have ye received the Holy Ghost since ye believed? And they said unto him, We have not so much as heard whether there be any Holy Ghost. And he said unto them, Unto what then were ye baptized? And they said, Unto John's baptism."
If sanctification and justification were received at the same moment, then this question is ridiculous.

At Corinth, Paul found a company of believers and asked, "Have ye received the Holy Ghost since ye believed?" This scripture alone is enough to prove that the infilling of the Holy Ghost occurs after we believe. The foregoing texts also are adequate to show that we can be saved and not yet be filled with the Spirit.

1. The apostles expected the believers to be filled. Note Paul's question.
2. Being saved from sin but not filled with the Spirit leaves one short of the power to perform effective service.
3. Jesus commanded, "Don't try to serve until you are 'endued' with power."

Thus, sanctification is not received at the altar of repentance, and yet we are commanded to receive the Spirit before attempting service.

Sanctification Is a Consecration

Reaching back into the Old Testament tabernacle service, we have God's illustration of sanctification. God gave Moses specific instructions on the building of the tabernacle in the wilderness. Every detail was outlined, and no deviation from that outline was tolerated.

Hebrews 8:5 says, "Who serve unto the example and shadow of heavenly things, as Moses was admonished of God when he was about to make the tabernacle: for, See, saith he, that thou make all things according to the pattern shewed to thee in the mount."

Moses was to follow the building plan exactly as God explained. Moses then built the building with two chambers. One chamber was for the priests to perform their service, and the other was for God Himself to occupy. Moses then built the altars. The brazen altar, the altar of burnt offering, was placed just inside the tabernacle entrance. The only way into the sanctuary was through this altar. This was the altar for sin. Inside the tabernacle just before the curtain leading into the holiest, or the place of God's presence, Moses built the golden altar, the altar of incense. The only way into the holiest was through the golden altar. Moses then made the furniture and implements, dishes, bowls, candlesticks, tables, altars, and so on. After all was completed, sacrifice was made, blood was administered to the altars, and everything pertaining to the tabernacle was "sanctified" or dedicated for the Lord's use. Dedicating or consecrating something to the Lord means giving it to the Lord for His use. Once dedicated, it is no longer available for any other purpose. Moses could not take the candlestick out to light his path in the dark. It was not his to use. It now belonged to God. When we seek God for His infilling, we also must be properly prepared by sacrifice and the blood of Christ applied to our hearts before we qualify for the infilling.

Romans 12:1 says, "I beseech you therefore, brethren, by the mercies of God, that ye present your bodies a living sacrifice, holy, acceptable unto *God*, which is your reasonable service."

When we bow at the brazen altar of repentance, our sins are canceled and our conscience is purged. This is justification. When we place our lives on the golden altar of service, we are consecrating our lives to God. And once we have done that, we are no longer our own, but dedicated to the service of God. Many people fail of this grace because they cannot or will not fully surrender to the will of God. They can bow at the altar of repentance for forgiveness of sin, but they cannot bow at the golden altar of self-sacrifice and take their hands off their own lives and let God direct them. Yet the above scripture says that it is only our "reasonable service." Also, there is additional cleansing that occurs in sanctification that does not occur in justification. In justification, our sins are canceled. In sanctification, the carnal nature is purged and we become a vessel that God can occupy with His Spirit.

In 2 Timothy, it says, "Nevertheless the foundation of God standeth sure, having this seal, The Lord knoweth them that are his. And, Let every one that nameth the name of Christ depart from iniquity. But in a great house there are not only vessels of gold and of silver, but also of wood and of earth; and some to honour, and some to dishonour. If a man therefore purge himself from these, he shall be a vessel unto honour, sanctified, and meet [worthy] for the master's use, and prepared unto every good work" (2 Timothy 2:19-21).

James talks to us about having a double mind. By this he means that some have a desire to serve God yet still want their own way. Until we can release our self-will, we are not fit for deeper service to God.

James 1:8 says, "A double-minded man is unstable in all his ways." And James 4:8 says, "Draw nigh to God, and he will draw nigh to you. Cleanse your hands, ye sinners; and purify your hearts, ye double minded."

Here the sinner, the unregenerate, is commanded to cleanse his hands of sinful deeds. He does this at the brazen altar of repentance. The double-minded man, the regenerated, is commanded to purify his heart or his carnal nature at the golden altar of consecration for service to God. Until this consecration is made, James marks him as unstable in all his ways. He will waver, he will be untrustworthy, and he will fail in temptation and be subject to all sorts of carnal attributes. This is because of the sinful nature inherent to humanity. Justification cleanses the hands or committed sins; sanctification purges the nature to restore us to the image of God as God intended in the creation.

It is important to comprehend the purpose of the tabernacle in the wilderness that Moses erected and the purpose of the spiritual grace known as sanctification. The tabernacle that Moses built in the wilderness contained two rooms. The first room was called the "holy place," and the second room was called the "holiest or most holy" place. The first room was for the priests to do service, replacing the shew bread, replacing oil in the lamp stand, burning incense on the golden altar, and so forth. The second room was occupied by the Ark of the Covenant and the mercy seat. The Mercy seat was a covering above the ark with two cherubim facing one another and looking over the ark. It is also the place where God dwelled among the people of Israel. It was the place of God's habitation. God's purpose was to be able to dwell in the midst of His people.

Before God could occupy the holiest place, the entire tabernacle and its contents had to be "sanctified." *Sanctification* in this context means "consecrated to the Lord's service." Every piece of furniture, and all the vessels, altars, candlesticks, and so on had to be specifically dedicated to the Lord. Once dedicated, all those items belonged to God, not the people. Never again could those items be used for any purpose other than the service of God in the tabernacle.

Ephesians 2:20-22 says, "And are built upon the foundation of the apostles and prophets, Jesus Christ himself being the chief corner stone; In whom all the building fitly framed together groweth unto an holy temple in the Lord: In whom ye also are builded together for an habitation of God through the Spirit."

A sanctified life is one that has been *cleansed of committed sin*. Once the blood has been applied for forgiveness of sins, the life is dedicated and consecrated to God without reservation. This is when the Spirit of God can occupy the heart. Remember, God wants to dwell within His people. Under the Old Testament, that dwelling was in the tabernacle. In the New Testament that dwelling is within the heart of the believer.

John 14:17 says, "Even the Spirit of truth; whom *the world cannot receive*, because it seeth him not, neither knoweth him: but ye know him; for he dwelleth with you, and shall be in you."

God's plan is to bring His people into such a relationship that they become a. habitation of God through the Spirit It is impossible for a sinful man to enter into the presence of God, and it is impossible for God to occupy a corrupt heart. Because of these impossibilities, first Christ cleanses the heart of the guilt of sin and then the Holy Spirit purifies the carnal nature. It is then and only then that God is free to enter the very soul of the believer. Here God is finally able to take up His rightful residence, His habitation, the Christian heart.

CHAPTER THREE

—⁘✦✦⁘—

Baptism

There are many approaches to the rite of baptism. Some feel that baptism is the entrance into the kingdom of God. Others consider it the door to the church. Membership is conferred upon people when the church baptizes them. Some baptize by sprinkling, others by dipping, and some by immersion. All insist that their mode of baptism is valid, biblical, and effectual for the purpose they believe baptism was ordained. Some will baptize infants, others will not. What is the Bible's rite of baptism? Do we sprinkle? Dip? Immerse? Do we baptize adults only or infants also? What does the Bible say about the matter?

Baptism in the Old Testament

From the beginning of national Israel, The Israelites practiced the rite of baptism, known to them as "divers washings." The laver was used for such washings for the priests and for certain parts of the sacrifices. People who were polluted for some reason were obliged to undergo certain washings. Washings were needed for ceremonial cleansing for such events as touching a dead person and those who were cured of leprosy. Such people were required to wash their clothes and their bodies. Some people were considered unclean for as short a time as an afternoon, and others were considered unclean for weeks. proselytes to the Jewish faith were baptized as a public testimony of their acceptance of the Jewish faith and promise to be obedient to the Law of Moses and so forth.

Baptism As a Rite of Moral Cleansing

Pilate practiced baptism when he washed his hands to symbolize his innocence in Christ's death: "When Pilate saw that he could prevail nothing, but that rather a tumult was made, he took water, and washed his hands before the multitude, saying, I am innocent of the blood of this just person: see ye to it" (Matthew 27:24).

Was it possible that washing the hands could erase moral guilt? Moral guilt cannot be erased by ceremoniously washing some part or even all of the body. Moral guilt is in the heart and remains after washing the external. Jesus explained this principle directly to the Pharisees. Jesus also exposed the Pharisees' internal corruption while they tried to appear clean on the outside, as we read in Matthew: "Woe unto you, scribes and Pharisees, hypocrites! for ye are like unto whited sepulchres, which indeed appear beautiful outward, but are within full of dead men's bones, and of all uncleanness" (Matthew 23:27).

Luke 11:37-39 says, "And as he spake, a certain Pharisee besought him to dine with him: and he went in, and sat down to meat. And when the Pharisee saw it, he marvelled that he had not first washed before dinner. And the Lord said unto him, Now do ye Pharisees make clean the outside of the cup and the platter; but your inward part is full of ravening and wickedness."

The truth of the matter is that external washings are simply that. Washing the outside of the flesh has no effect on the inward part of a person. True Baptism in the New Testament is a spiritual service rather than a ceremonial service as practiced in the Old Testament.

Infant Baptism

Baptizing babies has become commonplace for many of the formal denominations. Some actually believe that an infant is lost and doomed to eternal hellfire until it is baptized. Can a God of love and compassion, a God who sent Jesus Christ to suffer death in place of mankind, take an innocent baby and condemn it to eternal punishment without an opportunity to defend itself? What will we do with the stillborn? What about the millions of babies who are brutally murdered before they are born? How can we see them condemned to eternal hellfire? The truth is that the Bible does not teach us to baptize infants. John the Baptist made it very clear that there was a work to be done before the baptism:

> "But when he saw many of the Pharisees and Sadducees come to his baptism, he said unto them, O generation of vipers, who hath warned you to flee from the wrath to come? Bring forth therefore fruits meet [worthy of] for repentance" (Matthew 3:7-8).

John would not baptize one who had not repented properly. John's attitude indicates that he expected a change of heart before coming to him for baptism. Repentance means "a change of mind or direction." God has called on His people to repent and change their ways if they want to find His favor, according to 2 Chronicles 7:14: "If my people, which are called by my name, shall humble themselves, and pray, and seek my face, and turn from their wicked ways; then will I hear from heaven, and will forgive their sin, and will heal their land."

God promises to forgive their sin *after* they turn from their wicked ways. What wickedness have newborns done? What evil have infants committed? What sins can they turn away from? What do they know of sin, guilt, and responsibility? The apostle Paul explains the manner in which we become guilty of sin in Romans: "What shall we say then? Is the law sin? God forbid. Nay, I had not known sin, but by the law: for I had not known lust, except the law had said, Thou shalt not covet. But sin, taking occasion by the commandment, wrought in me all manner of concupiscence. For without the law sin was dead. For I was alive without the law once: but when the commandment came, sin revived, and I died. And the commandment, which was ordained to life, I found to be unto death. For sin, taking occasion by the commandment, deceived me, and by it slew me" (Romans 7:7-11).

Paul says that he was not conscious of sin until the law came. Before guilt of sin can be imputed, one must have knowledge of what sin is. Paul said, "I was alive without the law once." What he means is that he was *not* dead in trespasses and sins until he gained sufficient training in the law. Once he became old enough to comprehend the meaning of "Thou shalt not covet," he became responsible for it and guilty of it. Paul says of that moment, "Sin revived and I died." Paul was spiritually alive during his infancy and early childhood. When he became knowledgeable about right and wrong, he became a sinner and needed salvation, and after repentance, he needed baptism. An infant with no knowledge of wrong and no sins committed cannot be held accountable for mortal sin. Where is the justice in holding infants accountable for sins unknown and uncommitted? But, you say, didn't David acknowledge that he "was altogether born and conceived in sin"? Yes, David said that. Sin is in the nature of humanity, and because of that nature, all come under the guilt of sin. Paul did not say that we have no sin; he said that our sinful nature is not imputed to us until we come to knowledge of what that sin is and the consequences for that sin.

As Romans 5:13 says, "For until the law sin was in the world: but sin is not imputed when there is no law."

Immersion

Strong's Greek English concordance defines the Greek definition of the word translated as *baptize* means to "dip," "immerse," "baptisma (bap'-tis-mah); from NT:907; immersion, baptism (technically or figuratively)." The practice of sprinkling is necessary if we are going to baptize infants. Obviously, no mother is going to allow a minister to take her days-old child and plunge it into water. So, the mode of sprinkling was used as a method of baptizing babies. The definition for the word translated as *baptize* means to "dip" or "immerse." Baptism has a very special application to the Christian life. Baptism is our dying and resurrection with the Lord, as we read in Colossians 2:12: "Buried with him in baptism, wherein also ye are risen with him through the faith of the operation of God, who hath raised him from the dead."

Romans 6:4 says something similar: "Therefore we are buried with him by baptism into death: that like as Christ was raised up from the dead by the glory of the Father, even so we also should walk in newness of life."

When the body dies, we bury it deep in the ground. Making the grave too shallow would invite the stench of putrefying flesh to seep up through the ground. We also know that in the general resurrection the body will rise again. However, the same process occurs in the spiritual sense as the "old man" dies and the "new man" is reborn. Jesus told us to "take up our cross" and follow Him. Well, when Jesus took his cross, He went to Calvary. When we take up our cross, the first stop is Calvary for sins forgiven through the blood of Jesus Christ. On that cross, we also are crucified with Him.

Romans 6:6 says, "Knowing this, that our old man is crucified with him, that the body of sin might be destroyed, that henceforth we should not serve sin."

Being crucified, the "old man" dies and must be buried. Baptism is symbolic of that burying, captured in the words Buried with Him in baptism and risen with Him. Baptism is symbolic of the death of the old man (sinful) and the resurrection of the new man (righteous). Peter also makes it clear that baptism does not wash away sins.

"The like figure whereunto even baptism doth also now save us not the putting away of the filth of the flesh, but the answer of a good conscience toward God,) by the resurrection of Jesus Christ" (1 Peter 3:21).

Baptism by Peter's explanation does not "wash away the filth of the flesh" (sin), but it is "the answer of a good conscience before God." Baptism is our witness and testimony to the world that Christ has transformed our lives, forgiven us our sins, and cleansed us from all unrighteousness. We have a "good conscience" toward God.

CHAPTER FOUR

Modesty

Those of us who can remember back fifty or sixty years remember that most of the fundamental churches had some very strict standards on dress and Christian conduct. Although most of our fundamentalist churches imposed a well-balanced standard of attire, some, in their attempt to stand out with some degree of visible holiness, went beyond the standards of the Bible, imposing unreasonable restrictions and demands and creating what we call in the church "legalism" or "fanaticism." Because of the carnal nature of man that has been allowed to enter the churches, most of the churches have "let down" those standards practiced by earlier generations, claiming that "we are more enlightened and have greater liberty." Today, you can enter almost any church and see miniskirts, trousers, and blouses or dresses without sleeves and with plunging necklines. And, in some places, even shorts and tank tops. The Bible has very specific instructions on Christian attire, and if we are going to honor God and His Word, we need to accept and comply with the Word of God. You might ask then, "What are the standards of the Bible?" Simply stated, the Bible standard for attire is "modest apparel."

The first point is to define modesty. *Funk & Wagnall's New Comprehensive International Dictionary* defines the word *modesty* as follows: "decent reserve and propriety, Delicacy, Decorum, Bashfulness, Constraint, Shyness, Timidity, Shrinking from notice without assignable reason, a humble estimate of oneself in comparison with others. **Antonyms:**

Abandon, Arrogance, Boldness, Conceit, Haughtiness, Indiscretion, Sauciness, Etc." There are other definitions, but these are sufficient to establish that modesty is not a brazen exhibition of the human body.

Let us go right to the Bible.

First Timothy 2:9-10 says, "In like manner also, that women adorn themselves in modest apparel, with shamefacedness and sobriety; not with broided hair, or gold, or pearls, or costly array; But (which becometh women professing godliness) with good work."

And 1 Peter 3:3-5 says, "Whose adorning let it not be that outward adorning of plaiting the hair, and of wearing of gold, or of putting on of apparel; But let it be the hidden man of the heart, in that which is not corruptible, even the ornament of a meek and quiet spirit, which is in the sight of God of great price. For after this manner in the old time the holy women also, who trusted in God, adorned themselves, being in subjection unto their own husbands."

The above scripture references are describing the biblical standard for women to adorn themselves for appearing in public. We will discuss men later. In the first scripture, the terms *modest apparel, shamefacedness and sobriety* are used. *Shamefacedness* means "embarrassment," and *sobriety* means "self-restraint." Women today are no longer embarrassed if part of their body should become exposed, and with the way clothing and bathing-suit styles have developed, there certainly is no self-restraint. We also need to understand the difference between men and women as to what causes them to lust one for another. Men are visual and women are aural. Men are stimulated by what they see, and women are stimulated by what they hear. Therefore, a man is aroused to lust after a woman if he can see suggestive curves, hints of flesh, and subtle movements. On the other hand, most women are not aroused by nudity in men but aroused when men speak sweet nothings in their ears. Jesus made it clear that sexual intercourse was forbidden outside of marriage. But Jesus also told us that it is not necessary to commit an act of sexual intercourse to be guilty of adultery or fornication. A man becomes guilty when he fantasizes and lusts after a woman in his heart. With the brazen way that women dress today, with plunging necklines, short skirts, and short shorts I shouldn't have to describe the unholy bathing attire, a man has little chance to escape lustful thoughts.

Matthew 5:27-28 spells it out: "Ye have heard that it was said by them of old time, Thou shalt not commit adultery: But I say unto you, That whosoever looketh on a woman to lust after her hath committed adultery with her already in his heart."

When our women and young girls dress in a provocative fashion, they are causing the men and boys to look on them. They want to be sexy. Women need to understand that if a man is guilty for simply looking and lusting, the woman is likewise guilty of causing the man to fornicate with her in his heart and as such, is equally guilty in his fantasy. The question might be asked, What then is proper attire? Proper attire is "modest apparel": Clothing that does not provocatively accentuate the female body. A skirt or dress sufficiently long so as not to cause a man to seek another angle in hopes of seeing farther up the hemline. A neckline that does not expose a cleavage, and sleeves long enough that the blossoming of the breast is not visible when she raises her arms. Proper dress is clothing loose enough for the form and curves not to be excessively accentuated. Tight sweaters, skirts, and pants all accentuate the breasts, hips, and legs, and in many cases, actually outline a woman's underwear. All such dress is designed to draw the attention of the man, creating lust in him, and both man and woman become guilty. She is guilty when she dresses thusly, and he is guilty when he surrenders to his lustful fantasies. The term *shamefacedness* is used in the scripture referenced above. Throughout most of mankind's history, exposing the body to the opposite sex created a great sense of shame and embarrassment. Today, many of our women and young girls parade our beaches wearing only a G-string. Why are we shocked when our young girls are molested, raped, and worse?

The clothes that a woman wears are not the only issues addressed in the Bible's definition of *modest apparel*. There are the adornments that enhance one's beauty. Bracelets, earrings, necklaces, brooches, and pins are all designed to draw attention to the wearer. In one of the scriptures referenced above, Paul tells women to avoid adorning themselves with the following:

1. **Broided hair**
   This is hair with strands of gold intertwined.
   A modern application of this trend might be hair streaked with various colors, bleached, dyed, or styled in some outrageous manner.

2. **Gold, or pearls, or costly array**
   This refers simply to jewelry in general.
   Peter says basically the same thing: Whose adorning let it not be that outward adorning of plaiting the hair, and of wearing of gold, or of putting on of apparel.

Paul caps off his admonition by saying, "But (which becometh women professing godliness) with good work." We also have scripture in Old Testament prophecy saying that in the day of Christ that is today, godly women will no longer use costly adornments.

Isaiah 3:18-23 says, "In that day (the gospel day) the Lord will take away the bravery of their tinkling ornaments about their feet, and their cauls, and their round tires like the moon, The chains, and the bracelets, and the mufflers, The bonnets, and the ornaments of the legs, and the headbands, and the tablets, and the earrings, The rings, and nose jewels, The changeable suits of apparel, and the mantles, and the wimples, and the crisping pins, The glasses, and the fine linen, and the hoods, and the veils."

Because women are not stimulated by what they see in the way that men are, the mode of man's dress, although not likely to cause a woman to "lust" after him, is still critical. Like the woman, a man ought not to expose his body provocatively. A man does have body parts that can be enhanced with tight clothing. One way that men are going wrong today is in their use of clothing or adornments that are considered as being for women. Men are wearing long hair, necklaces, earrings, and suchlike. Although these adornments are discouraged in the Bible, we also recognize that they are feminine in nature, and if wearing them is considered prideful in women, it is shameful in men. See, for instance, the following biblical passages:

> "Know ye not that the unrighteous shall not inherit the kingdom of God? Be not deceived: neither fornicators, nor idolaters, nor adulterers, nor *effeminate*, nor abusers of themselves with mankind" (1 Corinthians 6:9).

> "The woman shall not wear that which pertaineth unto a man, neither shall a man put on a woman's garment: for all that do so are abomination unto the Lord thy God" (Deuteronomy 22:5).

God created mankind as men and women. The man is not to dress or act as a woman, and the woman is not to dress and act as a man. As we can see, the Bible has much to say about the way the godly dress and adorn themselves, and the biblical standard is to be simply attired so as not to exhibit a sense of pride, lust, and gaudy promotion.

CHAPTER FIVE

Christian Perfection

Many offer excuses for failure such as "nobody's perfect" or "I'm only human." Although it is true that we are weaklings at best and come short of all that is called holy, there is a power in man from God that raises him above the frailties of the flesh. Scriptures pertaining to perfection treat the subject both ways. The following scriptures are adequate proof that there is a Christian condition called "perfection." These passages talk of those "that are perfect." Some scriptures admonish us to "be" perfect, whereas others talk about "becoming" perfect. Here are some examples:

> 1 Corinthians 2:6: "Howbeit we speak wisdom among *them that are perfect*: yet not the wisdom of this world, nor of the princes of this world, that come to naught."

> 2 Corinthians 13:11: "Finally, brethren, farewell. *Be perfect*, be of good comfort, be of one mind, live in peace; and the God of love and peace shall be with you."

> Ephesians 4:13: "Till we all come in the unity of the faith, and of the knowledge of the Son of God, unto a perfect man, unto the measure of the stature of the fulness of Christ."

Philippians 3:15: "Let us therefore, as many as be perfect, be thus minded: and if in any thing ye be otherwise minded, God shall reveal even this unto you."

Colossians 1:28: "Whom we preach, warning every man, and teaching every man in all wisdom; that we may present every man perfect in Christ Jesus."

Colossians 4:12: "Epaphras, who is one of you, a servant of Christ, saluteth you, always labouring fervently for you in prayers, that ye may stand perfect and complete in all the will of God."

2 Timothy 3:17: "That the man of God may be perfect, thoroughly furnished unto all good works."

Hebrews 13:20-21: "Through the blood of the everlasting covenant, Make you perfect in every good work to do his will, working in you that which is wellpleasing in his sight, through Jesus Christ; to whom be glory for ever and ever. Amen."

James 3:2: "For in many things we offend all. If any man offend not in word, the same is a perfect man, and able also to bridle the whole body."

1 Peter 5:10: "But the God of all grace, who hath called us unto his eternal glory by Christ Jesus, after that ye have suffered a while, make you perfect, stablish, strengthen, settle you."

Paul also helps us to understand that perfection is a developing condition.

Philippians 3:12: "Not as though I had already attained, either were already perfect: but I follow after, if that I may apprehend that for which also I am apprehended of Christ Jesus."

What then is Christian perfection? Has any Christian achieved so high a degree of holiness that he cannot grow any better? We acknowledge that we are frail creatures at best. We are human, with all the fears and limitations of this body of flesh. No one has ever reached such a spiritual state that there is no more growing to be achieved. From that standpoint, we stand with Paul in declaring that "we have not already attained, neither were already perfect," but we press onward and upward. Such acknowledgment is no excuse for sin or other moral failure. Perfection is not achievable by human struggle. Perfection has two applications.

First, perfection is in the eye of the judge. A mother watching her young child scribble on a piece of paper sees artistic perfection where others see scribble. The special birthday card her five-year-old drew will stay in her treasure chest forever. The work is perfect because it is the best that the child is capable of. God calls men to turn from sin to holiness, from wrong to right. The new convert is seen as a "babe" in Christ. See, for instance, the following passages:

> "For every one that useth milk is unskilful in the word of righteousness: for he is a babe" (Hebrews 5:13).

> "And I, brethren, could not speak unto you as unto spiritual, but as unto carnal, even as unto babes in Christ" (1 Corinthians 3:1).

> "As newborn babes, desire the sincere milk of the word, that ye may grow thereby" (1 Peter 2:2).

As a babe, can one be expected to have the same spiritual maturity as one who has followed the Lord for a lifetime? No, there is learning to obtain, experience to gain, and faith, strength, and endurance in the Christian walk. Like the child, these spiritual babes will make mistakes and foolish decisions, and fall prey to many blunders. But, like the mother with her five-year-old, God looks on the achievements of His children in the light of their knowledge. When a child of God performs to the best of his ability, God rewards that person the same as He does the more capable. In the parable of the talents, God gave the older, experienced servant five talents to invest. Another servant was not so proficient, and God gave him only two talents. The least experienced He gave only one talent. He expected them all to do their best in their investments. The first two servants doubled their respective investments, and the Lord gave them both the same reward. Although one had gained five talents and the other only two, they were both perfect in their performance of the respective duties.

Matthew 25:20-23 says, "And so he that had received five talents came and brought other five talents, saying, Lord, thou deliveredst unto me five talents: behold, I have gained beside them five talents more. His lord said unto him, Well done, thou good and faithful servant: thou hast been faithful over a few things, I will make thee ruler over many things: enter thou into the joy of thy lord. He also that had received two talents came and said, Lord, thou deliveredst unto me two talents: behold, I have gained two other talents beside them. His lord said unto him, Well done, good and faithful servant; thou hast been faithful over a few things, I will make thee ruler over many things: enter thou into the joy of thy lord."

So, we see that Christian perfection is performing to the best of our ability, walking in all the light that we have, and being obedient to all that we know.

Second, there is a far deeper meaning for Christian perfection. Perfection is not simply proficiency in talents or abilities. Neither is perfection simply the art of being good, kind, and loving. Christian perfection is a condition of the heart. When God created humankind, He made him a morally responsible creature. That is, he had the power of choice, he had conscience, he had knowledge of right and wrong, and he was responsible for choosing the right path in life. While Adam was still a lump of mud, God breathed into his nostrils the breath of life and Adam became *a* living soul. Having a soul means that there is a vital connection between the Creator and the created. Not only did Adam have a soul, but the breath of God also put the spirit of life into the man. This special "life" was not simply the animation of movement, but a "living" within the creature's life. Adam was created in the image of God Himself. Holy, sinless, eternal, "perfect"—all the attributes that are God were infused into Adam. One of those attributes was the "Spirit of life." This Spirit of life is the essence of the Spirit of God, and when Adam chose to sin, the Spirit of life could no longer reside within his heart. Thusly, the man had a void in his heart that left him thirsting for spiritual communion and after a few generations, men forgot the God of creation and began to make other gods for themselves. Man *must* have a god. If he cannot find the true God, he will make an idol. The man *must* worship something in an attempt to fill the void in his heart. The only thing that will fill that void is the Spirit of God, restoring the spiritual condition of the man to the condition God breathed into Adam in the creation, "the breath of life." Jesus prepared His disciples for this "breath" just before His departure from this life. Jesus "breathed" on them.

It says in John 20:22, "And when he had said this, he breathed on them, and saith unto them, Receive ye the Holy Ghost."

On the day of Pentecost, the Holy Ghost was given to all the disciples gathered in that upper chamber, and their lives were changed forever. Peter, the failure, was transformed into a powerhouse who boldly stood before the very murderers of the Lord and declared, "It was you who put the Lord of glory to death." The power of God within him broke the hearts of the hearers who begged "men and brethren, what must we do?" Jesus also had told His disciples not to enter their labors in the gospel until they had received the power described above. "And, behold, I send the promise of my Father upon you: but tarry ye in the city of Jerusalem, until ye be endued with power from on high" (Luke 24:49).

The apostle Paul tells us that we must grow in our Christian experience and reach for perfection: "Therefore leaving the principles of the doctrine of Christ, let us go on unto perfection; not laying again the foundation of repentance from dead works, and of faith toward God" (Hebrews 6:1).

Many people genuinely want to serve the Lord but do not understand that having our sins forgiven is not the end of our salvation. Paul also tells us in Romans 5:1-2 that once we have received justification, we have the opportunity to gain access into the very presence of God himself, or, better yet, God dwelling in us.

First we are justified, saved, at peace with God: "Therefore being justified by faith, we have peace with God through our Lord Jesus Christ" (Romans 5:1).

Second we have access into standing grace, after we are justified: "By whom also we have access by faith into this grace wherein we stand, and rejoice in hope of the glory of God" (Romans 5:2).

Therefore, Christian perfection is the restoration of God's work of creation in returning to us, the image of God, holy, sinless, loving, righteous, *perfect.*

CHAPTER SIX

The Holy Life

Romans 12:1 says, "I beseech you therefore, brethren, by the mercies of God, that ye present your bodies a living sacrifice, *holy*, acceptable unto God, which is your reasonable service."

We might ask ourselves, "Why is it that men refuse to measure up to the standard of God's holiness?" The answer is very simple. It is because of the carnal nature of humanity without God's transforming power. The above scripture clearly says that it is only our "reasonable" service to give our lives in living service to the Lord. The life that we offer to God is to be a life that is *holy*, fully redeemed and ready for service.

God declared the people of Israel in the wilderness to be a holy people because He is a holy God.

Leviticus 11:45 says, "For I am the Lord that bringeth you up out of the land of Egypt, to be your God: ye shall therefore be holy, for I am holy."

Leviticus 20:7-8 says, "Sanctify yourselves therefore, and be ye holy: for I am the Lord your God. And ye shall keep my statutes, and do them: I am the Lord which sanctify you."

Simply being the chosen people of God did not make them holy. They were to be holy by obedience to the Word of the Lord. In any generation, God has demanded only that degree of holiness that was in keeping with their knowledge of the will or commandments of God. By modern standards we could condemn nearly all of the holy men of the Old Testament. Noah gave himself to drunkenness. Abraham lied and placed his wife's life in jeopardy to save his own. Isaac did the same thing. David committed adultery and murder and yet is considered "a man after God's own heart." God's judgment of them was according to their obedience to their knowledge of God's commandments to them. During the period of the Old Testament, men in times of spiritual leanness gave themselves to idolatry. Many of the kings are commended as "doing that which was right in the sight of the Lord." Yet many of these same kings did not remove all the abominations from their land. Their spiritual understanding was not perfectly clear, and they were judged according to their understanding.

Acts 17:30 says, "And the times of this ignorance God winked at; but now commandeth all men everywhere to repent."

In the New Testament dispensation we do not have such latitude in the performance of the Christian life. The above scripture clearly tells us that the Old Testament saints because of their ignorance of true holiness were excused. "God winked at their ignorance." That tolerance is not available today because we have the living Word, the Lord Jesus Christ, and the Word of God coupled with the spirit of knowledge.

First Corinthians 12:8 says, "For to one is given by the Spirit the word of wisdom; to another the word of knowledge by the same Spirit." And Ephesians 1:17 says, "That the God of our Lord Jesus Christ, the Father of glory, may give unto you the spirit of wisdom and revelation in the knowledge of him."

Although God "winked" at our Old Testament counterparts, He commands us to "repent." Like the people of the Old Testament, we are responsible only for the knowledge that we have. However, God has revealed His word so clearly that we can no longer claim ignorance, as we learn in Romans 1:18-20: "For the wrath of God is revealed from heaven against all ungodliness and unrighteousness of men, who hold the truth in unrighteousness; Because that which may be known of God is manifest in them; for God hath shewed it unto them. For the invisible things of him from the creation of the world are clearly seen, being understood by the things that are made, even his eternal power and Godhead; so that they are without excuse."

Any person attempting to present himself at the judgment with sin on his life will have no excuse or defense.

Matthew 22:11-13 says, "And when the king came in to see the guests, he saw there a man which had not on a wedding garment: And he saith unto him, Friend, how camest thou in hither not having a wedding garment? And he was speechless. Then said the king to the servants, Bind him hand and foot, and take him away, and cast him into outer darkness; there shall be weeping and gnashing of teeth."

At the Jewish wedding, each of the invitees was furnished a "wedding garment." In the above scripture, the man who presented himself at the wedding uninvited or without a wedding garment was not questioned further. No excuse was accepted. He was bound and cast into outer darkness, "lost forever." For you and me, the wedding garment is that robe given to every repentant heart that has accepted the Lord Jesus Christ as Lord and master. The wedding garment is the "robe of righteousness" given to us at the time that the blood of Jesus washes away the filth of the flesh.

When Adam found he and his wife were "naked," it was the removal of the covering of innocence that brought them shame. They had been covered with the "robe of righteousness" until they sinned. With their sin came the removal of their spiritual covering, and they saw their nakedness and were ashamed. That spiritual nakedness that exposed Adam's guilt remains on the hearts of all Adam's posterity and the need for a re-covering becomes apparent.

Romans 5:13-15 says, "For until the law sin was in the world: but sin is not imputed when there is no law. Nevertheless death reigned from Adam to Moses, even over them that had not sinned after the similitude of Adam's transgression, who is the figure of him that was to come. But not as the offence, so also is the free gift. For if through the offence of one many be dead, much more the grace of God, and the gift by grace, which is by one man, Jesus Christ, hath abounded unto many."

Second Corinthians 4:18 says, "While we look not at the things which are seen, but at the things which are not seen: for the things which are seen are temporal; but the things which are not seen are eternal."

Second Corinthians 5:1-5 says, "For we know that if our earthly house of this tabernacle were dissolved, we have a building of God, an house not made with hands, eternal in the heavens. For in this we groan, earnestly desiring to be clothed upon with our house which is from heaven: If so be that being clothed we shall not be found naked. For we that are in this tabernacle do groan, being burdened: not for that we would be unclothed, but clothed upon, that mortality might be swallowed up of life. Now he that hath wrought us for the selfsame thing is God, who also hath given unto us the earnest of the Spirit."

Although the above scriptures are referring to our heavenly home and glorified body, a closer examination will show that there is also a tabernacle to be obtained in this life. In the reference above, 2 Corinthians 4:18, the apostle is referring to things "not seen," things accepted by faith, not by sight, looking for things "spiritual." In these verses, Paul tells us that we have a heavenly tabernacle—a house "not made with hands," "eternal in the heavens." Paul further says that we "earnestly desire *to be clothed upon with our house which is from heaven.*" Paul goes on to say that he wants to be "clothed" so that he will not be found "naked," as we have seen earlier; being clothed or unclothed is dependent on the covering of God for sin. We also found that the soul attempting to approach judgment without said covering had no excuse and was cast out (Matthew 22:1-14). If we are to successfully face the shock of judgment, we must be "clothed upon" before our arrival at the judgment bar of God. Paul concludes the above scripture by showing us that it is God that has "wrought" in us that transforming nature or cleansing Spirit as "He hath given us the earnest of the Spirit."

The "earnest" of the Spirit is the Holy Spirit of God. In any legal transaction, an "earnest deposit" is required for the transaction to be legal and binding. In our heavenly transaction, God has made a "unilateral" contract with us. A unilateral contract is one that is binding on the offeror, but conditional on the offeree. God has made the offer of salvation and perfect soul cleansing through the offering of the Lord Jesus Christ as our atonement for sin. With this offer of salvation is the promise of eternal life. God made the offer and set the conditions for the acceptance of that offer. When man complies with the terms set forth by God, God must honor His contract.

God's conditions for His offer are basically simple but clearly demanded.

1. Accepting by faith the atoning sacrifice of the blood of Jesus Christ
2. Forsaking all sin and filth of the flesh
3. Accepting holiness (see the chapter on sanctification)

Consider the following scriptures:

> "Even the righteousness of God which is by faith of Jesus Christ unto all and upon all them that believe: for there is no difference" (Romans 3:22).

> "He that committeth sin is of the devil; for the devil sinneth from the beginning. For this purpose the Son of God was manifested, that he might destroy the works of the devil. Whosoever is born of God doth not commit sin; for his seed remaineth in him: and he cannot sin, because he is born of God. In this the children of God are manifest, and the children of the devil: whosoever doeth

not righteousness is not of God, neither he that loveth not his brother" (1 John 3:8-10).

"Follow peace with all men, and holiness, without which no man shall see the Lord" (Hebrews 12:14).

Part of the conditions of God's contract of salvation is that men cease committing sin and take on holiness that is living (Christ-like) lives.

In First Peter, we read, "Because it is written, Be ye holy; for I am holy" (1 Peter 1:16).

Holiness is one of the attributes of God, and the object of God's plan for man is to be restored to the "image" of God as in the beginning of the creation. Man was made in God's own image, possessing all of God's attributes: sinless, pure in heart, holy, perfect, eternal, and so on. Jesus came to remove the sin from the lives of His people and to make them clean of fleshly pollutions. Lies, hatred, vulgarity, strife, deception, slander, and a host of carnal attributes are not God-like and are not acceptable attributes in the life claiming to be holy. True holiness is a life exhibiting the attributes of God. That "old" carnal nature that we call "the old man" must be cleansed and purged from the heart to make room for the Spirit or nature of God in the heart of His believers. Jesus also commanded His disciples to "tarry in Jerusalem until they had been endued with power from on high."

Luke 24:49 says, "And, behold, I send the promise of my Father upon you: but tarry ye in the city of Jerusalem, until ye be endued with power from on high."

John 14:16-17 says, "And I will pray the Father, and he shall give you another Comforter, that he may abide with you for ever; Even the Spirit of truth; whom the world cannot receive, because it seeth him not, neither knoweth him: but ye know him; *for he dwelleth with you, and shall be in you.*"

When Jesus was preparing to leave His followers and return to His Father, He promised them another comforter that *had* been *with* them, but *will* be *in* them. The spirit of the Father had been *with* them in the presence and person of Jesus. The spirit of the Father will be *in* them in the presence of the indwelling Holy Spirit of God.

We began with a pure heart and must end with a pure heart. The seed of sin planted by Satan was not Adam's intent. We cannot blame him for the thoughts introduced by another. So, the seed of carnal desire was planted. When Adam ate the forbidden fruit, its seed blossomed into sin and Adam died spiritually and was destined to die physically. The fall was a two-step process. Adam first had the desire to sin and then committed the sin. The return also is a two-step process. First the sin must be eradicated by the atoning power of the blood of Jesus Christ. Then, the heart is purified by the power of the Holy Spirit. So many people attempting to live the Christian life fail to achieve a true "victorious" life because they fail to "go on unto perfection."

Hebrews 6:2 says, "Therefore leaving the principles of the doctrine of Christ, let us go on unto perfection; not laying again the foundation of repentance from dead works, and of faith toward God."

The foundation of repentance is that carnal nature that causes men to sin in the first place. Although the blood of Christ cancels committed sin, the Christian who does not deal with the carnal nature abiding in his members will soon find his will at war with the will of God. Such a war is destined to failure because of the conflict between the desire to do right and the hunger to do wrong. Paul describes this conflict as a wretched condition.

Romans 7:23-24 says, "But I see another law in my members, warring against the law of my mind, and bringing me into captivity to the law of sin which is in my members. O wretched man that I am! who shall deliver me from the body of this death?"

A holy life is one that is pure not only in deeds done in the body, but also the motives and ambitions of the heart. The evil "carnal" nature being removed from the heart leaves an acceptable dwelling place for the Spirit of the Lord. God cannot and will not occupy a carnal heart. He declared Himself to be a "jealous" God and will not share His sovereignty with other gods. Not even the gods of the flesh.

Many professing Christians in this day and time are accepting a way of life that is not consistent with biblical holiness. The Bible commands us to leave the world and follow Jesus, as we see in the following verses:

> "If ye were of the world, the world would love his own: but because ye are not of the world, but I have chosen you out of the world, therefore the world hateth you" (John 15:19).

> "Love not the world, neither the things that are in the world. If any man love the world, the love of the Father is not in him" (1 John 2:15)

> "Behold, what manner of love the Father hath bestowed upon us, that we should be called the sons of God: therefore the world knoweth us not, because it knew him not" (1 John 3:1).

The general Christian world today has forsaken the counsel of spiritual leaders of the past for a more liberal standard of life declaring that they have grown in understanding. Consider where this new understanding has taken us. Our churches are filled with alcoholics claiming salvation. Many denominations are changing their tenets to accommodate homosexual members, homosexual marriages, and even ordination of homosexual pastors. Couples living together without the sanction of marriage have no shame when bowing at the communion table. Pastors who molest children are not charged with sin but actually defended. Young people overwhelmed in their passions are counseled in behavior rather than led to repentance. Because of this changing attitude toward sin, streets that were relatively safe sixty years ago today are a battleground. No neighborhood is exempt from the mobile gun battles of street gangs. Almost everyone has been subjected to the violation of the thief. Our beaches and public swimming pools are filled with bathing costumes that leave nothing to the imagination. Modesty is a subject that cannot be preached in most pulpits because the pastor would lose much of his congregation. Vulgar gyrations on the dance floor are actually conducted in many church fellowship halls.

With so much compromise with sin in the hearts of the professing religious world, Satan has taken advantage of such an opportunity and has moved his attack to the legal system. Our lawmakers have become so liberal that they attempt to eliminate God completely from our society. Prayer was eliminated from our schools. Public buildings can no longer display Christian themes. There has been the suggestion that we remove "In God we trust" from our currency. The early immigrants to this country were the Puritans, who fled their native land to escape such religious tyranny for religious liberty. The founding fathers of our nation believed and declared that it would be impossible to establish and govern a nation such as ours without the guidance of Almighty God. By no stretch of the imagination can anyone consider the people and conditions described in the last two paragraphs as examples of holy living. We have succeeded in our spiritual decline as to find ourselves "reprobate" before God.

Romans 1:28 says, "And even as they did not like to retain God in their knowledge, God gave them over to a reprobate mind, to do those things which are not convenient."

True holy living and the holy life can only be described as "God-like." Can anyone honestly think that God Himself would engage in such practices described above? A genuine Christian truly living a holy life cannot practice such behavior since he would not be living like God. Therefore the holy life is truly a "godly" life: honest, loving, gentle, kind, without malice or hatred, pure in mind and heart, humble, and all the attributes that make up the person we call God. The reason that so few people actually live a holy life is that they do not know God. No life really changes from evil to good without the influence of God *in* the heart. A true holy life is a life that has been infilled with a Holy God. A holy life is one where God is a living resident in the heart. The mind of God is implanted into the mind of the believer.

Philippians 2:5 says, "Let this mind be in you, which was also in Christ Jesus."

Such a heart does not struggle to assert its own will but is submissive to the will of God. Such a heart does not search for ways to justify moral failure, but willingly repents and turns from sin. Such a heart desires to please God in every way and will avoid any thing or condition not approved of God. God does not approve sin, and sin is impossible to conquer without the Spirit of God resident in the heart of the Christian believer. The absence of the Spirit of God in the heart is a fundamental reason why much of modern religiosity is so destitute of morality. The heart without God is a cesspool of foul pollution.

Jeremiah 17:9 says, "The heart is deceitful above all things, and desperately wicked: who can know it?"

Man cannot cleanse or purge his own heart of such pollutions, but God can. Jesus came to restore the human heart to the spiritual condition that God intended when He created the first man. That man was created in "His own image"—that is, he possessed all the attributes that are God: pure, sinless, holy, perfect, eternal, and so on. Adam was blessed with a special gift not given to any other of God's created creatures. God breathed into Adam's nostrils and he became a living soul (Genesis 2:7). Prophetically, wind and breath are descriptions of the Spirit of God. Remember when Jesus was preparing to depart this life and return to heaven, He breathed on his disciples and said to them, "Receive ye the Holy Ghost" (John 20:22). The breath of God implanted into Adam was God's Holy Spirit. When Adam sinned, the breath of life departed from his heart and Adam died the spiritual death and became a sinful and guilty man of the world. He was no longer God-like, no longer "holy," and no longer "in the image of God." The Spirit had departed. To truly live a holy life, one must again receive the breath of life. *"Receive ye the Holy Ghost."*

Any Christian who genuinely wants to live a holy life pleasing to God must let God do a complete work in his or her heart. If we will obey God's Word and seek His full salvation, we will submit our hearts to Jesus for the application of the sin-cleansing blood. We will also surrender our wills to the purifying power of the Holy Spirit so that the will of God can replace our own. Full salvation is a two-step process:

1. Our sins are forgiven.
2. Our carnal nature is cleansed, making the way for the Holy Spirit to again occupy the human heart.

God will not occupy a polluted heart. With the pollution gone, the Holy Spirit again takes up residency in the heart and the Christian is restored to the "image of God." (See the chapter on sanctification.) With God in the heart and the mind of Christ governing our lives, sinful things no longer attract, and we can "walk with God."

Romans 5:1-2 says, "Therefore being justified by faith, we have peace with God through our Lord Jesus Christ: By whom also we have access by faith into this grace wherein we stand, and rejoice in hope of the glory of God."

We began this chapter with the following scripture:

> "I beseech you therefore, brethren, by the mercies of God, that ye present your bodies a living sacrifice, holy, acceptable unto God, which is your reasonable service" (Romans 12:1).

Notice that the verse admonishes us to offer ourselves as a "living" sacrifice, which is our "reasonable" service. In Jewish sacrifices, the gift was brought to the priest who took the offering and placed it on the altar, where it was consumed. To satisfy the command "Be ye holy," we must place our lives on the altar of personal sacrifice to be used by God for His purposes. When such an offering is made, our lives become God's to be used to fulfill His will and purpose, and never again is it ours. We give the life to Him, He fills it with Himself, Christ's mind merges with ours, and we become holy. This holiness is only our "reasonable" service.

CHAPTER SEVEN

⸻⊹❦⊹⸻

The Sinless Life

Men are ever looking for an excuse for human weakness or failure. We just do not want to confess that we are responsible for our actions. A popular entertainer and comedian during the 1960s constantly used the phrase "The devil made me do it." Although it is true that the devil is behind all evil thought and action, we are not excused from personal responsibility. Eve in the garden would never have tasted the fruit of the Tree of Knowledge of Good and Evil if Satan had not tempted her. Although it was Satan who planted the seed of desire in her heart, she chose to believe Satan's enticing words over the command of God and became a guilty soul. Eve then became the instrument of enticement for her husband and Adam became a guilty soul. Did the devil make them do it? *No.* The devil only suggested with his lies. They believed those lies and violated the Word of the Lord and became guilty by their own actions; they cannot blame anyone. They could not even blame Satan, because they could have refused to follow his advice.

Much of our modern religion provides a dishonest heart with many avenues to soothe the conscience from accusations. We have thousands of churches, religions, and beliefs. You can worship God, Allah, Satan, rocks, stars, and any other object that you choose. There will be a church or religious group that will agree with you and set any condition or standard of life that will permit any action you wish. There is a religion for every concept of human behavior, including vulgarity of speech, immorality, and even murder. We have religions that will permit you to be a member in good standing while you continue to lie, steal, deceive, cheat, slander, and a host of other wicked human practices. These are all the natural tendencies of man without God.

In the creation, God formed man from the dust of the earth. He was nothing more than an earthly form of life. God took an extra step with Adam that He did not with any other species of life. God placed within the man not only the animation of life, but also a living spirit, as it says in Genesis: "And the Lord God formed man of the dust of the ground, and breathed into his nostrils the breath of life; and man became a living soul" (Genesis 2:7).

It is the "breath" of God, which is the Spirit of God, that made Adam a "living soul." God placed within the man a piece of Himself, and while that spirit remained a living part of Adam's life, Adam was happy and content and enjoyed the wonders of paradise or Eden. When Adam sinned, that Holy Spirit departed from his heart and he knew guilt, fear, and shame. He knew he was naked because the clothing of righteousness had been removed and he was alone with the guilt of sin. It is in this "breath of life" in the human being where God made provision for Himself, a place for His Spirit to reside in the heart of the man. God created the man with a spirit tied to Himself. It is this special spiritual tie that makes man a moral creature and so responsible for violating the Word of God.

Man's spiritual nature makes him a higher form of creation than all other creation, and the Spirit of God in the heart is necessary for him to be complete. When the Spirit of the Lord left Adam's heart, there remained an emptiness that required filling. Any student of history will notice that men have always felt the need for a deity. Every society, nation, or people has had its gods. All the Middle Eastern countries of antiquity had their gods. Explorers to the New World found that every colony or tribe of people had their gods. Discoverers of the remote and uncharted islands of the sea found people who avidly worshipped their gods. As recently as the twentieth century, colonies of people were found who had never had contact with the rest of the world and also had an active system of worshipping their gods. Man cannot escape his need for God. God placed a "compartment" for Himself in the heart of man, a compartment that *must* be filled. If the God of heaven is absent, men will fill that void with something else, even if he has to make his gods for himself; the emptiness *must* be filled.

Man, without God, is basically stupid and cannot create a god better than himself. Since man without God is of an evil nature and subject to the basest of human degradation, the gods that the man creates will be of the same nature. Therefore the man submits himself to serve gods of anger, violence, revenge, and a host of other evil attributes. Man will mutilate himself for these gods. He will sacrifice the fairest of the community or even his own children to these gods.

Deuteronomy 18:10 says, "There shall not be found among you any one that maketh his son or his daughter to pass through the fire."

The above scripture refers to the practice of placing children as a sacrifice into the arms of the idol of Molech. These arms extended over a fire that consumed whatever or whoever was placed in those arms. Can you imagine a mother taking her baby and walking up to this ugly and terrifying idol, placing her baby on those blistering hot arms, and watching the child scream and writhe in agony as it burns to death? Such is the requirement of the gods that man creates for himself.

Left to ourselves, we are hopelessly wicked, corrupt, and at the mercy of our own senses, which can travel in no direction but into deeper wickedness. That old cliché "No man can pick himself up by his own bootstraps" is so true. Try it sometime. Take hold of your shoelaces and lift with all your might. How high did you get? Silly, isn't it? And yet this is exactly what man is trying to do spiritually. Unfortunately, men cannot deny their deeds. No matter how we try to atone for ourselves, the hands that committed the sinful deed are still attached to our arms, and we remain guilty of all the unholy thoughts and actions of our past. The problem that we face is that because God placed a sense of conscience within our hearts, we are painfully aware of a need for atonement. We turn over a new leaf. We make promises, commitments, and resolutions, all to no avail, because the only one who can resolve the conflict, God, is absent from the heart. Remember that God created a compartment in your heart for Himself.

If the presence of God in the heart is so vital to our sense of well-being, why did God depart? God was and is unable to remain a resident in the sinful heart.

Habakkuk 1:13 says, "Thou art of purer eyes than to behold evil, and canst not look on iniquity." And Exodus 33:20 says, "And he said, Thou canst not see my face: for there shall no man see me, and live."

The above scriptures indicate two things. First, God cannot look favorably on an evil heart filled with iniquity. Second, man cannot look on a holy God while he is filled with iniquity and live. So, we see that while man is in a sinful condition, he cannot look on God and God cannot look on him. There is no greater illustration of this principle than the crucifixion of Christ. While Jesus hung on the cross, God had to turn His face away from him for a portion of the time, as we read in Matthew 27:45-46: "Now from the sixth hour there was darkness over all the land unto the ninth hour. And about the ninth hour Jesus cried with a loud voice, saying, Eli, Eli, lama sabachthani? That is to say, "My God, my God, why hast thou forsaken me?"

In Jesus's entire life, He had never been spiritually separated from His Father. For a soul who has never known spiritual abandonment, this event came as a shock. It is true that He was aware of all that was to befall Him, yet who can truly be prepared for the sudden abandonment of God? During the hours of noon till three in the afternoon, Jesus was under the cloud of darkness. God was not able to look on Him and Jesus was unable to sense the presence of His Father as He became sin for the world. Jesus not only died in the agony of the flesh, but died the death of separation from God, the agony of a lost soul—the terror every soul not filled with His spirit will face.

Second Corinthians 5:21 says, "For he hath made him to be sin for us, who knew no sin; that we might be made the righteousness of God in him."

Isaiah 53:5-6 says, "But he was wounded for our transgressions; he was bruised for our iniquities: the chastisement of our peace was upon him; and with his stripes we are healed. All we like sheep have gone astray; we have turned every one to his own way; and the Lord hath laid on him the iniquity of us all."

God's plan to save a sinful world was to take the only one that was sinless, Himself in the office of the Son, and transfer the guilt of mankind to Him and then make Him pay the penalty for sin, which is death, according to Romans 6:23, which says, "For the wages of sin is death."

Once a sinful deed is done, it cannot be denied or revoked. It is a recorded fact, and all the words of forgiveness will not erase the reality that the deeds were done. When Jesus went to the cross, He received the iniquity of us all and became our propitiation for sin. Having received our guilt, God, who is of "purer eyes," could no longer look on Jesus, and so darkness prevailed from noon until three in the afternoon. Jesus endured the physical suffering, but the spiritual suffering, (feeling alone and without God) finally overwhelmed Him, and He cried out, "My God, my God, why hast thou forsaken me?" Jesus had assumed or taken our guilt to Himself, and being now covered with our guilt, paid the price for sin, which is death. When we accept the sacrifice of Christ for our atonement, we become participants in the Crucifixion. Our old sinful nature is laid on Him and we pay the penalty of death for sin through Jesus Christ.

Romans 6:6 says, "Knowing this, that our old man is crucified with him, that the body of sin might be destroyed, that henceforth we should not serve sin."

And Romans 6:4 says, "Therefore we are buried with him by baptism into death: that like as Christ was raised up from the dead by the glory of the Father, even so we also should walk in newness of life."

The principle of "putting off the old man and putting on the new man" suggests that the guilty "old man" is no longer living. While this body continues to live, the old sinful nature is dead and we have become a "new creature."

Consider 2 Corinthians 5:17, which says, "Therefore if any man be in Christ, he is a new creature: old things are passed away; behold, all things are become new."

It is this "becoming" a new creature, or as I prefer, a "new creation," that frees us from the old penalty for sin, because that "old man," the guilty one, is dead and we are with Christ, resurrected from that dead sinful nature and become a new creation.

Why is it then that modern religion makes such allowance for sin? It is because their "old man" is not dead. Religious movements and denominations have so compromised the Word of God that religious people can do all the things the world does and still hold on to their profession and remain in "good standing" with their church. They can drink, curse, smoke, chew, dance, attend ungodly movies, surf the pornographic Internet, read *Playboy,* and wear immodest attire. When they fall into sexual immorality, they are counseled rather than exposed for what they really are, sinners. Is it any wonder that our world is in such deplorable condition? We seem to want to blame our politicians for the moral decline in our nation, but the truth of the matter is that they are only a symptom of the problem. The true failure lies with the Christian ministry that has allowed such corruption to enter the church and the hearts of the people, and as the people go, so goes the nation.

The Bible has zero tolerance for sin. Let's look at some of the scriptures:

> "Whosoever *committeth sin transgresseth also the law: for sin is the transgression of the law*. And ye know that he was manifested to take away our sins; and in him is no sin" (1 John 3:4-5).

> "He that committeth sin is of the devil; for the devil sinneth from the beginning. For this purpose the Son of God was manifested, that he might destroy the works of the devil. *Whosoever is born of God doth not commit sin*; for his seed remaineth in him: and *he cannot sin*, because he is born of God" (1 John 3:8-9).

> "Be not deceived: evil communications (behavior) corrupt good manners. Awake to righteousness, and *sin not; for some have not the knowledge of God: I speak this to your shame*" (1 Corinthians 15:33-34).

> "And he that doubteth is damned if he eat, because he eateth not of faith: for whatsoever is not of faith is sin" (Romans 14:23).

> "The thought of foolishness is sin: and the scorner is an abomination to men" (Proverbs 24:9).

> "For out of the heart proceed evil thoughts, murders, adulteries, fornications, thefts, false witness, blasphemies" (Matthew15:19).

> "Then when lust hath conceived, it bringeth forth sin: and sin, when it is finished, bringeth forth death" (James 1:15).

> "And have no fellowship with the unfruitful works of darkness, but rather reprove them" (Ephesians 5:11).

"But exhort one another daily, while it is called To day; lest any of you be hardened through the deceitfulness of sin" (Hebrews 3:13).

"Righteousness exalteth a nation: but sin is a reproach to any people" (Proverbs 14:34).

"Thou hast set our iniquities before thee, our secret sins in the light of thy countenance" (Psalm 90:8).

"Come now, and let us reason together, saith the Lord: though your sins be as scarlet, they shall be as white as snow; though they be red like crimson, they shall be as wool" (Isaiah 1:18).

"For her sins have reached unto heaven, and God hath remembered her iniquities" (Revelation 18:5).

"For though thou wash thee with nitre, and take thee much soap, yet thine iniquity is marked before me, saith the Lord God" (Jeremiah 2:22).

Do not the above referenced scriptures settle the question of sin in the heart? By the Word of God we see that sin will never enter into heaven and stand in the presence of God, and neither will a sinful heart. Sin and those practicing sin will have their place in the "lake of fire."

The Bible is filled with scripture describing a principle of life called holiness. If we are to be able to stand in the presence of God, we must be rid of the condition that separated man in the first place. Since sin cannot come into God's presence, those who will approach Him must be clear of sin. The intended spiritual condition of man is that God is a resident in the heart of man. There is a special place in the heart of the man that God made for himself when He created the first man. Man is incomplete without the Spirit of God residing in his heart. Yet, God cannot occupy a heart already occupied by sin. This is the reason for the principle of the old man, new man. Before God can and will occupy our heart, it must be clean of all unrighteousness. Too, the heart that brings sin into itself effectively drives the Spirit of God out. There is no cohabitation of God with carnal flesh. Obviously, if sin cannot enter the presence of God, our soul must be cleansed from sin. And, since we cannot remove our sin by denying it, we must apply God's formula for its removal. Do not be deceived: any sin remaining in your life will meet you at the judgment bar of God.

First Timothy 5:24 says, "Some men's sins are open beforehand, going before to judgment; and some men they follow after."

Every man's sin will be presented at the judgment. Those who place their trust in the shed blood of the Lord Jesus Christ will not meet their sins, because their sins have already gone to judgment with Jesus in His atoning sacrifice on the cross of Calvary, and the penalty for sin has already been paid. But those souls who reject the atoning power of the blood of Jesus find that their sins follow after them and confront them before the throne of God, and they will stand guilty as charged. If you are among those who have not had the blood applied to your heart, the gates of heaven will not open for you! But the gates of hell will be open wide. *Beware.*

CHAPTER EIGHT

The Church

Throughout the Greek world and right down to New Testament times, *ekklesia* was the word defining the regular assembly of the whole body of citizens in a free city-state The Hebrew word *qahal*, which in the Old Testament denotes the "congregation" or community of Israel, especially in its religious aspect as the people of God. In this Old Testament sense we find ekklesia employed by Stephen in the book of Acts, where he describes Moses as "he that was in the church." We see here three basic definitions for the term *church*.

1. Calling the assembling of all the citizens of a community for a public forum
2. The congregation as used above includes all the members related to one another.
3. The assembling of those members related to one another

None of the above definitions refer to a building, organization, or physical structure. Rather, they refer to people bound together by a form of society. To the Greeks the word referred to all the citizens of a community. To the ancient Hebrews, it referred to all the members of the twelve tribes of Israel. To the Christians it referred to all the members of the family of God. There are many references in the New Testament to the church at some location or city or in someone's home. See, for instance, the examples below.

"Unto the church of God which is at Corinth, to them that are sanctified in Christ Jesus, called to be saints, with all that in every place call upon the name of Jesus Christ our Lord, both theirs and ours" (1 Corinthians 1:2). In this scripture those included are the "sanctified," saints, and those who claim Jesus as Lord and have submitted their earthly will to His heavenly will.

"Paul, an apostle of Jesus Christ by the will of God, and Timothy our brother, unto the church of God which is at Corinth, with all the saints which are in all Achaia" (2 Corinthians 1:1). In this scripture those included are "all the saints," whether in Corinth or the surrounding communities.

"The churches of Asia salute you. Aquila and Priscilla salute you much in the Lord, with the church that is in their house" (1 Corinthians 16:19). In this scripture those included are the members of the family and friends of Aquila and Priscilla. In every case we are talking about people and not physical locations. The location of the church is unimportant. What is important is that the people of God are the church. Their meeting place is only the location where the church assembles. This congregation includes all believers, whether in Corinth, Jerusalem, or Los Angeles. The church is not bound by location, time, or distance. Jesus, in John 10:16, indicates that there are people who have not as yet believed on Him. Through the centuries, Jesus has been calling these sheep, and when they heed His call, they are included in the church, as we read in John 10:16: "And other sheep I have, which are not of this fold: them also I must bring, and they shall hear my voice; and there shall be one fold, and one shepherd."

The apostle Paul does not restrict the family of God to any place or time, but includes every believer whether living or dead, on earth or in heaven: "For this cause I bow my knees unto the Father of our Lord Jesus Christ, Of whom the whole family in heaven and earth is named" (Ephesians 3:14-15).

It is easy to see by definition and by biblical usage that the term *church* identifies the whole of all the saved of any place or time and that none are excluded. Why is it then that we have so many "churches," all different in name and doctrine and all claiming to be the one Bible church? All these churches claim to be preaching the truth, and yet in many cases they are preaching a doctrine totally opposite one from the other. How can two people or churches preaching contrary doctrine both be right? The prophet Amos understood the principle of unity when he said, "Can two walk together, except they be agreed?" (Amos 3:3).

God never has identified with more than one people. In ancient times, He put His name in Israel. God allowed Gentiles to come into the Jewish faith, but never did He take a Gentile nation to identify with, nor did He approve of the people of God joining or affiliating with a Gentile nation. There were only one people of God, and Jehovah was known as the God of the Jews. When Jesus established the church, he made it clear that it was His church, not churches. "I will build my church; and the gates of hell shall not prevail against it" (Matthew16:18).

It seems we need to learn the same lessons over and over again. The primary principle that we have forgotten is how God has His church organized. I think we all remember how God organized the church in the wilderness. God called Moses, commissioned him, and sent him to bring His people out of the land of Egypt. God told Moses how to build the Tabernacle. God told Moses how to order the sacrifice and worship service. God told Moses how to assemble the congregation around the Tabernacle. God also admonished Moses to be careful about building according to the pattern that God gave him. "And look that thou make them after their pattern, which was shewed thee in the mount" (Exodus 25:40). In other words, God organized and directed the church. Moses had no part in the decision process. Moses, like all the prophets who came after him, spoke the Word of the Lord: nothing more, nothing less.

When Israel wanted a king to be like the other nations, they went against the will of God in placing another ruler over themselves in place of the Lord, as we see in these passages from First Samuel:

"And said unto him, Behold, thou art old, and thy sons walk not in thy ways: now make us a king to judge us like all the nations" (1 Samuel 8:5).

"And the Lord said unto Samuel, Hearken unto the voice of the people in all that they say unto thee: for they have not rejected thee, but they have rejected me, that I should not reign over them" (1 Samuel 8:7).

When Jesus established His church, He did not share the headship or rulership of the church with anyone. "For the husband is the head of the wife, even as Christ is the head of the church: and he is the Savior of the body" (Ephesians 5:23). Although the apostles developed some organization for delegating the work, they did not organize themselves as a governing body, usurping the authority that belongs to Jesus alone. As time passed, men became carnal in heart, desiring to have dominance over others, and pastors or bishops of larger congregations began to exercise authority over smaller congregations. Jesus was very clear when He told His disciples that such authority was not to be exercised among them.

Mark 10:42-43 says, "But Jesus called them to him, and saith unto them, Ye know that they which are accounted to rule over the Gentiles exercise lordship over them; and their great ones exercise authority upon them. But so shall it not be among you: but whosoever will be great among you, shall be your minister."

Man in his arrogance actually rose to the position as to declare himself "the head of the church." The popes of Rome have and still make such representation. By making such a declaration, he reduced himself to the place of having to govern the church without divine guidance. God has never relinquished His authority over the church, and when a body of ministers assign this authority to themselves, they, like Israel so long ago, have rejected the Lord from ruling over them and are on their own, having to govern in their own wisdom, which will fail every time. Thus, we have a period in history known as the Dark Ages because of the spiritual darkness of the era. "If the blind lead the blind, both shall fall into the ditch" (Matthew 15:14).

We have seen reformations, restorations, and revivals that were brief times when spiritual men recognized that God ruled the church through the Holy Spirit. Such men humbled their hearts and surrendered themselves into the hand of God and accepted divine leadership. Although these times of revival are recorded in history, we again seem to forget who is in charge, and again we set up religious movements ruled by men. Our intentions may have some validity. "We want to hold on to the foundations of our forefathers." "We want to move out into new light." "We want to revert to the teachings of earlier times." We can recite many reasons for establishing a new movement, but the result always seems to be the same. We set up a hierarchy of authority declaring who is in and who is out based on how they measure up to our regulations, and we become no better than what we came out from.

Membership in the church has always been the same. In ancient Israel, membership in the Jewish faith came through being born into a Jewish family. Converts could enter into Jehovah worship through conversion to the Jewish faith. Membership in the New Testament church is by the same means: being born into the family of God. Joining a church by signing a membership application or agreeing to abide by its tenets is nothing less than idolatry, which is spiritual adultery. By joining an earthly church organization, we again choose to place another king over us. Jesus will never relinquish His headship over His church. Jesus also declared, "I will build my church; and the gates of hell shall not prevail against it" (Matthew 16:18). Therefore, any organization where man admits or rejects membership is **not the church of God**. God's church has only one mode of membership, and that is the "new birth."

Consider these passages:

> "Jesus answered and said unto him, Verily, verily, I say unto thee, Except a man be born again, he cannot see the kingdom of God" (John 3:3).

> "But now hath God set the members every one of them in the body, as it hath pleased him" (Acts 2:47).

> "And the Lord added to the church daily such as should be saved" (1 Corinthians 12:18).

How dare any man or organization claim to be God's church when they limit their membership by some rule of authority even though God alone has the authority to induct members into His church? God puts the members in when they are "saved," "born again." You must be a member of the family of God to be a member of the Church of God.

The church is also identified as the "Body of Christ."

> "For as we have many members in one body, and all members have not the same office: So we, being many, are one body in Christ, and every one members one of another" (Romans 12:4-5).

> "Now ye are the body of Christ, and members in particular" (1 Corinthians 12:27).

Our modern sectarian churches for the most part recognize that God has a universal church. The Bible identifies that church as the Church of God. Most of the churches have no problem recognizing that name as the Body of Christ, and they think of themselves as a member or branch of that Body. The problem with that theory is that of unity. In the natural body there is total harmony and sympathy between the various members of the body. If my leg is injured, my hands will bind it up. I will obtain crutches or some other assistance to relieve the trauma until the leg gets well. It is *my* leg and without it I am out of balance and limited in functionality. The sectarian churches are not in harmony with one another. Although they attempt to have joint ventures with one another, there is no fundamental unity because of the exclusiveness of their membership practices and the differences in their doctrine. Those who belong to the ABC church do not belong to the XYZ church. The ABC church accepts members who are baptized by their ministry. The XYZ church accepts members by signing a pledge to adhere to the tenets of the church and support it with finance. The URN church requires a course of training and confirmation at the Communion table. We learned earlier that none of these modes of entrance into the church will work since God alone inducts the members as they are saved. It is possible to become a member of these churches without ever experiencing the "new birth." Likewise there are differences in doctrine. The ABC church teaches one thing. The XYZ church preaches another, and the URN church believes something totally different altogether. If all these church "branches" were "of the body," they would be controlled by the head and would all be speaking the same thing.

First Corinthians 1:10 says, "Now I beseech you, brethren, by the name of our Lord Jesus Christ, that ye all speak the same thing, and that there be no divisions among you; but that ye be perfectly joined together in the same mind and in the same judgment."

How can so many churches preach and practice so many things contrary one to the other and contrary to the Word of God and still honor the above scripture? It is impossible. There is no true harmony, and since Christ is *not* divided—"Is Christ divided? was Paul crucified for you? or were ye baptized in the name of Paul?" (1 Corinthians 1:13)—those practicing divisive religion are not the Church of God.

There are many groups calling themselves the Church of God. *Church of God* is the true Bible name for the Church that Jesus said He would build when He said, "I will build my church; and the gates of hell shall not prevail against it" (Matthew 16:18), and not all who call themselves the Church of God are allowing Christ to be its head. When a group of congregations bind together and exclude all others and fail to cooperate, they may claim that they are the Church of God, but they are nothing more than another denomination. Evidence of rejecting Christ as head is in the fact that they have accepted a man or group of men to stand between the congregation and the Lord Jesus Christ. (Thus saith the pastor, thus saith the ministry.) Whatever happened to "Thus saith the Lord"?

Consider the following passages:

> "Take heed therefore unto yourselves, and to all the flock, over the which the Holy Ghost hath made you overseers, to feed the *church of God*, which he hath purchased with his own blood" (Acts 20:28).

> "Unto the *church of God* which is at Corinth, to them that are sanctified in Christ Jesus, called to be saints, with all that in every place call upon the name of Jesus Christ our Lord, both theirs and ours" (1 Corinthians 1:2).

> "Give none offence, neither to the Jews, nor to the Gentiles, nor to the *church of God*" (1 Corinthians 10:32).

> "What? have ye not houses to eat and to drink in? or despise ye the *church of God*, and shame them that have not? What shall I say to you? shall I praise you in this? I praise you not" (1 Corinthians 11:22).

> "For I am the least of the apostles, that am not meet to be called an apostle, because I persecuted the *church of God*" (1 Corinthians 15:9).

> "Paul, an apostle of Jesus Christ by the will of God, and Timothy our brother, unto the *church of God* which is at

Corinth, with all the saints which are in all Achaia" (2 Corinthians 1:1).

"For ye have heard of my conversation in time past in the Jews' religion, how that beyond measure I persecuted the *church of God*, and wasted it" (Galatians 1:13).

"(For if a man know not how to rule his own house, how shall he take care of the *church of God*?)" (1 Timothy 3:5).

"Salute one another with an holy kiss. The churches of Christ salute you" (Romans 16:16).

The preceding scriptures should be enough for any reasonable thinker to prove that "Church of God" is the name recognized in the Bible and that this name honors the Lord and acknowledges Him as the Head. For any religious body to identify themselves by another name has very serious implications in the Bible. In the book of Revelation we have a prophetic overview of the panorama of the gospel day. This panorama begins with the establishing of the church at Pentecost and ends with the final judgment and eternal reward or punishment. Among the letters to the seven churches we have a letter addressed to the church in Philadelphia. Although there were seven churches in Asia Minor at the time of the apostles, these churches to which Christ addressed His letters are prophetically seven separate and successive periods of time throughout the gospel day. Philadelphia was the sixth church and represents a period of unrestrained revival. Philadelphia is a church, or a period in which the church is in full cooperation with Christ and the Holy Spirit is at liberty to direct within it. One very important commendation that Jesus pays this church is that they recognized and used the name Church of God. "I know thy works: behold, I have set before thee an open door, and no man can shut it: for thou hast a little strength, and hast kept my word, and hast not denied my name" (Revelation 3:8). God has always declared Himself to be a jealous God, as seen in this passage from Exodus:

"Thou shalt not make unto thee any graven image, or any likeness of any thing that is in heaven above, or that is in the earth beneath, or that is in the water under the earth: Thou shalt not bow down thyself to them, nor serve them: for I the Lord thy God am a jealous God, visiting the iniquity of the fathers upon the children unto the third and fourth generation of them that hate me" (Exodus 20:4-5).

We have mentioned before that God will not share or relinquish His rule of authority over His people or His church. When men organize themselves into the various factions that we call the denominations, they are creating divisive bodies or groups in which members are contained and governed by some ministerial assembly or committee and in some cases, by a single man or woman. Establishing these sectarian boundaries is nothing less than fencing in the members, separating them one from the other and thus destroying the unity of the Body of Christ by separating the members of His Body. Most Bible scholars recognize that the name Babylon as used in the Revelation is referring not to that ancient city but to the Babel of confusion of the many doctrines of the sectarian community. We have so many churches preaching so many different doctrines, all different and many contrary one to another, that those looking for a place to worship are hard pressed to know which is right. This is confusion, Babel, and is identified in Revelation as Babylon.

Researching Bible history we remember that the southern kingdom of Judah was captured and carried away as prisoners to Babylon by Nebuchadnezzar, the king of Babylon in 606 BC. They were scattered throughout the Babylonian and Persian empires for seventy years when God called them out to return to Jerusalem and rebuild their temple and their city and restore themselves in Zion, the city in which God chose to place His Name. After the sixteenth-century Reformation launched by Martin Luther, history tells us the people of God were scattered throughout the multiplicity of churches that began to evolve, creating what the Bible calls a "cloudy and dark day"—a day that is unclear or cloudy spiritually because of the confusing doctrines preached among them.

Ezekiel 34:12 says, "As a shepherd seeketh out his flock in the day that he is among his sheep that are scattered; so will I seek out my sheep, and will deliver them out of all places where they have been scattered in the cloudy and dark day." (Please read the entire text of Ezekiel 34:1-13.)

The name Babylon has always been synonymous with confusion. When Nimrod built the tower of Babel shortly after the flood of Noah's time, God dispersed the people throughout the world by the confounding of their languages. Language is the unifying tie between all mankind. If we speak the same language, we have unity. If we don't speak the same language, we will leave the company of the ones around us and seek those with whom we can communicate. The same principle of language applies to the churches. Each church organization or denomination has its own fundamental doctrines that it holds. These individual doctrines are religious languages. It is because of the differing religious languages that people acquainted with one church will seldom feel comfortable in another.

God's people therefore have found themselves scattered throughout the Babel of sectarian division. As God called His people out of literal Babylon after their seventy years of captivity in 536 BC, God again is calling His people out of spiritual Babylon and back to Zion. In the Old Testament, Zion was Jerusalem, and in the New Testament, Zion is the church that Jesus built. What church is the church that Jesus built? Its name is Church of God. However, with so many denominations calling themselves the church of God, which one should we join? You cannot join the Church of God. Remember that it is God who sets the members in the Body (1 Corinthians 12:18). It is God who adds to the church daily such as should be saved. (Acts 2:47). If man can add your name to the church membership roster, it is not God's church. Jesus said that your names are written in heaven (Luke 10:20). The Church of God is the church that admits all the saved and preaches the "whole counsel of God." The Church of God is that church that is governed by the Lord Jesus Christ (Isaiah 9:6). The Holy Spirit is at liberty to "lead" not only the church and its ministry but also the individual members of the Body of Christ. The Church of God is that church where Jesus is its Head.

Revelation 18:1-5 says, "And after these things I saw another angel come down from heaven, having great power; and the earth was lightened with his glory. And he cried mightily with a strong voice, saying, Babylon the great is fallen, is fallen, and is become the habitation of devils, and the hold of every foul spirit, and a cage of every unclean and hateful bird. For all nations have drunk of the wine of the wrath of her fornication, and the kings of the earth have committed fornication with her, and the merchants of the earth are waxed rich through the abundance of her delicacies. And I heard another voice from heaven, saying, Come out of her, my people, that ye be not partakers of her sins, and that ye receive not of her plagues. For her sins have reached unto heaven, and God hath remembered her iniquities."

Many religious organizations were started with good intentions by concerned and caring men and women. They were people who saw their beloved church or denomination departing from the truth as they saw it. Spiritual leaders sought to keep their people from following a declining religion, so they began their own. However, man-governed institutions always eventually fall into the same trap because they are governed by men and not by God. New Testament Babylon includes the conglomeration of the sectarian or denominational systems, and God will not bless those organizations that build fences or walls around the people of God, which is nothing more than the dividing of God's people, which is sin. Sectarianism based on the above scripture is an abomination with God and has been rejected as a blessable part of His Body. The command therefore goes forth for the saved and enlightened Christians within the denominational systems to "come out of her."

What is her sin? Fornication! The church that Jesus built is His bride. For His bride to accept another head is spiritual adultery. An honest look into the denominational world will easily reveal that God no longer has any rule within it. We are constantly reading in our newspapers about one of our major denominations having to change their tenets to accommodate some moral adjustment because of the demands of the people or changes in our society that they are unable to deal with scripturally. When these changes occur, they normally will acknowledge the Bible teaches one thing, but they must make the changes anyway because of the demands placed upon them. The most prevalent of these alterations of doctrine at the time of this writing is the ordaining of homosexuals to the Christian ministry. The Bible is absolutely clear on the issue of homosexuality. It is perversion, it is abomination, and it is sin. The Bible's position is not disputed by these denominations, but they are making the adjustments despite the judgment of the Word of God. This practice of man changing the tenets of the Word of God is man taking the place of God, rewriting the Word of God, and as such we have spiritual adultery: man giving his heart and fidelity to another head. The scriptural doctrine pertaining to homosexuality is covered in another chapter of this book.

What then is the church? Although it is the most finely organized body ever assembled, it is not an organization. It is an organism. Jesus established it, Jesus governs it, and Jesus keeps it clean and pure. Since Jesus changes not, the church changes not. Centuries come and centuries go, but the church remains the same. The principles and doctrines outlined by the apostles are the principles and doctrines expected by God of His church today. Look at the following scriptures:

"For I am the Lord, I change not," says Malachi 3:6. (*God does not change.*)

"For unto us a child is born, unto us a son is given: and the government shall be upon his shoulder: and his name shall be called Wonderful, Counsellor, The mighty God, The everlasting Father, The Prince of Peace" (Isaiah 9:6).

> "And hath put all things under his feet, and gave him to be the head over all things to the church, Which is his body, the fulness of him that filleth all in all" (Ephesians 1:22-23).

> "Jesus Christ the same yesterday, and to day, and for ever" (Hebrews 13:8). (*Jesus does not change.*)

Likewise, the church does not change. The church is the body of the Lord Jesus Christ, and each born-again Christian is a member of that body. It is his body, not bodies.

First Corinthians 12:15-20 says, "If the foot shall say, Because I am not the hand, I am not of the body; is it therefore not of the body? And if the ear shall say, Because I am not the eye, I am not of the body; is it therefore not of the body? If the whole body were an eye, where were the hearing? If the whole were hearing, where were the smelling? But *now hath God set the members every one of them in the body, as it hath pleased him.* And if they were all one member, where were the body? But now are they many members, yet but one body."

Our denominational leaders may call on this scripture to prove that God recognizes denominational differences as different members of the body of Christ. However, the next scripture text identifies the various members as individuals and members in particular. Each member of the body—arm, leg, ear, and so on—has a particular purpose. Paul identifies some of these members as

1. Apostles
2. Prophets
3. Teachers
4. Members possessing particular gifts
   A. Miracles
   B. Healings
   C. Helps
   D. Governments
   E. Tongues

First Corinthians 12:27-29 says, "Now ye are the body of Christ, and members in particular. And God hath set some in the church, first apostles, secondarily prophets, thirdly teachers, after that miracles, then gifts of healings, helps, governments, diversities of tongues. Are all apostles? are all prophets? are all teachers? are all workers of miracles?"

At no time does Paul ever talk about differing organizations, and whenever he talks about the church, whether in Jerusalem, Corinth, or anywhere else, he is talking about the Church of God in the singular. If he uses the plural, he is referring to the various congregations of the church, not the organizations. But he is talking to the saints, individuals who make up the body of Christ. Paul brings the focus of the body as the community of the saints. Members of one household and "fellow citizens with the saints."

In Ephesians 2:19-22 we read, "Now therefore ye are no more strangers and foreigners, but fellow citizens with the saints, and of the household of God; And are built upon the foundation of the apostles and prophets, Jesus Christ himself being the chief corner stone; In whom all the building fitly framed together groweth unto an holy temple in the Lord: In whom ye also are builded together for an habitation of God through the Spirit."

This household is not built on some man's concept of spirituality, but on the foundation of the Word of God. "And are built upon the foundation of the apostles and prophets, Jesus Christ himself being the chief corner stone." The apostles represent the New Testament and the prophets represent the Old Testament. They are bound together by Jesus Christ, the chief cornerstone. Thus, Jesus' church is built on the whole Word of God, all the words of God spoken to Moses, the judges, the prophets, and the apostles, and by Christ. Any man who thinks he is wise enough to alter God's Word is placing his own soul in the fire.

Revelation 22:18-19 says, "For I testify unto every man that heareth the words of the prophecy of this book, If any man shall add unto these things, God shall add unto him the plagues that are written in this book: And if any man shall take away from the words of the book of this prophecy, God shall take away his part out of the book of life, and out of the holy city, and from the things which are written in this book."

Finally, as shown in, Ephesians 2:22, God has a particular purpose for the church that most religious people do not understand. "In whom all the building fitly framed together groweth unto an holy temple in the Lord: In whom ye also are builded together for an habitation of God through the Spirit." The church, which is the "kingdom of God," is for the habitation of God Himself. The purpose of the tabernacle in the wilderness was to have a place where God could set his presence among His people. The temple of Solomon was for the same purpose. Jesus made it clear where we would find this kingdom in the following verse: "Neither shall they say, Lo here! or, lo there! for, behold, the kingdom of God is within you" (Luke 17:22).

God no longer dwells in tents or temples made with hands, but in the hearts of His people, which is the church. All the tabernacles and beautiful buildings erected by man do not constitute the church. A single religious organization does not constitute the church, and in fact, all the religious organizations together throughout the world do not constitute the church. Ideas, beliefs, and doctrines of men do not constitute the church. The church is the sweet fellowship of the Father and the Son in the hearts of the Saints of God, men and women who truly have the Spirit of the living God abiding in their hearts. God draws kindred hearts together for the habitation of His Spirit. God walked with Adam in fellowship, and He also walks with His saints, who are the church of the living God.

CHAPTER NINE

Unity

John 17:20-21 says, "Neither pray I for these alone, but for them also which shall believe on me through their word; That they all may be one; as thou, Father, art in me, and I in thee, that they also may be one in us: that the world may believe that thou hast sent me."

Any general knows that if his army is to be victorious in battle, he must have perfect unity of purpose throughout his command. His lieutenants, sergeants, and foot soldiers must all be following the same orders with absolute commitment even unto death. He also knows that defeating an enemy can be assured if he can only disrupt and divide the enemy's will and purpose. Accusation and suspicion are greater weapons than cannon and mortars. Dividing and conquering was a tactic used by God to save King Jehoshaphat and give him victory against the armies of Ammon, Moab, and Seir (2 Chronicles 20:1-24). In this battle Ammon and Moab turned against Seir, and then they all turned on one another until they were all dead. When Jehoshaphat and his army arrived, the battle was already over. These enemies of Judah had become divided and were no longer an effective army, and had devoured one another.

Satan is a master at twisting the Word of God, causing people to interpret the Word in a human light. Jesus prayed that they (the disciples) might be ONE like He and the Father are ONE. This oneness is called unity, a bonding and binding together into a single organism, the church that Jesus built. Satan has revised the application to mean "union." This union is represented by the great variety of religious fellowships and denominations filling our world today. Although we acknowledge that much good has been done by many of the denominations, they remain earthly organizations originated by some man or group of men and governed by a head or headquarters. All power and authority within the denomination is vested in the ruling authority, whether a man, a committee, or a board of directors. God is not their head. The Word of God is not their authority, as we have seen in recent times in the changing of their tenets to reflect their opinion of the needs of the present generation. These adjustments many times are admittedly contrary to the Word of God, but they feel they have the authority to ignore God's Word in favor of their own judgments.

Among these denominations are a variety of beliefs, rules, doctrines, and modes of worship, many contrary one to the other. This is union, not unity, but it is man's way. When man loses the guidance of the Holy Spirit, he has no choice but to figure things out for himself, using human wisdom and judgment. When man usurps God's place in the governing of the church, he will fail every time. A Sunday school teacher was presenting a lesson on the origins of the denominations. She had outlined a tree showing Jesus as the trunk and the denominations as limbs and branches. The splintering denominations were assigned to their respective limbs and branches. A minister from the Church of God happened to be in the room and the teacher asked him, "I cannot figure out where to place the Church of God In what branch do you fit in the denominational tree?"
The minister replied, "Nowhere. I am a branch all by myself." Is it any wonder that our religious movements have lost their power to move God? A fundamental truth has been lost, and in its place is a divided religious world. This is not what Jesus had in mind.

Consider the following verses:

> "Jesus saith unto him, I am the way, the truth, and the life: no man cometh unto the Father, but by me" (John 14:6).

"I am the true vine, and my Father is the husbandman. Every branch in me that beareth not fruit he taketh away: and every branch that beareth fruit, he purgeth it, that it may bring forth more fruit" (John 15:1-2).

"If a *man* abide not in me, he is cast forth as a branch, and is withered; and men gather them, and cast them into the fire, and they are burned" (John 15:6).

"I am the vine, ye are the branches: He that abideth in me, and I in him, the same bringeth forth much fruit: for without me ye can do nothing" (John 15:5).

Every child of God is a branch in the vine and they should be *one* in Christ, the *vine.*

"And if a house be divided against itself, that house cannot stand" (Mark 3:25).

People in competition with one another strive to destroy. Division weakens anything it touches. Divide a nation and it can be conquered. Divide a home and the family is scattered. Divide a church and its influence is lost, its power is gone, miracles are rare, and bickering and backbiting is the result. It is a stench in the nostrils of God.

God intended Israel and the church to be one. The body of Christ ought to be in unity today. Jesus prayed that they may "all be one," indivisible.

First Corinthians 1:10 says, "Now I beseech you, brethren, by the name of our Lord Jesus Christ, that ye all speak the same thing, and that there be no divisions among you; but that ye be perfectly joined together in the same mind and in the same judgment."

God said of ancient Israel, "Yet I had planted thee a noble vine, wholly a right seed: how then art thou turned into the degenerate plant of a strange vine unto me?" (Jeremiah 2:21).

It is natural for God's people to be together.

We read in John 10:1-5, "Verily, verily, I say unto you, He that entereth not by the door into the sheepfold, but climbeth up some other way, the same is a thief and a robber. But he that entereth in by the door is the shepherd of the sheep. To him the porter openeth; and the sheep hear his voice: and he calleth his own sheep by name, and leadeth them out. And when he putteth forth his own sheep, he goeth before them, and the sheep follow him: for they know his voice. And a stranger will they not follow, but will flee from him: for they know not the voice of strangers."

It has been said that it is natural for sheep to graze together. They never divide themselves until something disturbs them, such as a lion, wolf, bear, or some such threat. When alarmed, they may scatter briefly, but then they come back together. The only way to keep a flock apart is to build a fence around them and keep them bottled up and separate from other sheep.

God's people are rightly called sheep. Jesus identifies Himself as the good shepherd. When the Prince of Peace, the one who is one with the Father and the one who is one with His people, comes into the hearts of the saints, there is a deep hunger for oneness with one another. The people of God will seek to identify with other members of the family of God.

Any flock or people can be disturbed. Misunderstandings, bad feelings, jealousy, strife, and so forth will naturally drive a wedge between people, groups, and congregations. Fellowship becomes impossible for a variety of reasons. Setting rules, standards, and regulations have wreaked havoc among the people of God. The ABC group cannot fellowship with the XYZ group because of differences in dress code or personal appearances. The LMN group cannot fellowship with the URN group because the pastors are at odds with each other. One gets a "revelation" or "vision" and tries to impose his views on others, rejecting those who "see not the light." Some will set rules or standards and require submission. Refusal to submit is considered rebellion and grounds for rejection. All the while God's people are scattered to the four winds.

A true child of God wants to be with the brethren. If a brother gets sick spiritually and separates himself from the brethren, there is a hungering in the saints for the return of the injured or wayward brother. When that brother returns, there is rejoicing at the reclamation of a soul. God's true people do not drive the weak brother away; they welcome him back into the fold and nurture him back to health. If we but break down the walls of separation, the flock naturally becomes one fold.

God condemns division.

Unity can be preached in a way that drives people apart. There is a wrong way to do a right thing. Many pastors have the notion that since they are the watchmen on the walls, they have special authority to direct and govern the people of God. They set guidelines and standards of practice and demand compliance. Legalistic preaching bruises tender hearts and drives away honest-hearted seekers. Although they view all this as keeping the body clean, these pastors are only building fences around their little flock and separating their people from all God's other people. Listen to the Lord's condemnation of such:

"Woe be unto the pastors that destroy and scatter the sheep of my pasture! saith the Lord. Therefore thus saith the Lord God of Israel against the pastors that feed my people; Ye have scattered my flock, and driven them away, and have not visited them: behold, I will visit upon you the evil of your doings, saith the Lord. And I will gather the remnant of my flock out of all countries whither I have driven them, and will bring them again to their folds; and they shall be fruitful and increase. And I will set up shepherds over them which shall feed them: and they shall fear no more, nor be dismayed, neither shall they be lacking, saith the Lord" (Jeremiah 23:1-4).

Unity is the natural result of God's love.

No child of God would intentionally divide himself from the saints. Many preachers are very intelligent and can quote Bible verse by the chapter and have deep training in theology, yet they have not comprehended that the Body of Christ is an organism and not an organization. That organism draws its very life not from any movement, church, assembly, or fellowship but from Jesus Christ Himself. He is the life flowing through the spiritual veins of the people of God. John 14:6 says, "I am the way, the truth, and the life." The people of God *are* the Body of Christ. That Body lives because Jesus lives, and the heart of Jesus Christ is implanted within the hearts of His people. As we accept the concept of the trinity of God the Father, Son, and Holy Spirit, we need to see that the same unity of the Father with the Son is also ordained to be the unity between the people of God.

> "And I have declared unto them thy name, and will declare it: that the love wherewith thou hast loved me may be in them, and I in them" (John 17:26).

> "And now I am no more in the world, but these are in the world, and I come to thee. Holy Father, keep through thine own name those whom thou hast given me, that they may be one, as we are" (John 17:11).

Can we not see in the preceding verses that the relationship of the people of God is akin to the relationship between Jesus and the Father? There is a binding of hearts through the kinship of the new birth into salvation by Jesus' shed Blood. Every child of God is kin to every other child of God. This is a truth any rational mind should be able to comprehend. The apostle John declares that our fellowship with one another is dependent on our fellowship with God. Note the following scripture, from 1 John 1:3: "That which we have seen and heard declare we unto you, that ye also may have fellowship with us: and truly our fellowship is with the Father, and with his Son Jesus Christ."

There is a test to determine if we are the children of God. I challenge all who practice division to measure themselves by the following scripture, from 1 John 3:14-15: "We know that we have passed from death unto life, because *we love the brethren*. He that loveth not his brother abideth in death. Whosoever hateth his brother is a murderer: and ye know that no murderer hath eternal life abiding in him."

The love of God in the Christian heart should be the same love that is residing in the heart of God. It is God's love that was willing to die for man's salvation. Ought not the people of God be willing to sacrifice for one another?

God prepared the perfect form of life when He established the family. He gave Adam a wife and a family was born. He identified Himself as a husband to Israel. Jesus identified Himself as a husband to His people, the church or the Bride of Christ.

Pastors are set as shepherds of the people and are commissioned to preach the gospel, which is the sharing of the love of God. Many preach a unity that actually separates the saints by declaring that only they are right, and all others are wrong. They consider themselves "the Body." When several groups each indentify themselves as "the Body," my question to them is, How many bodies does Christ have? Only human arrogance will think that only they are in favor with God. Many profess unity but reject those with differing opinions. Remember Jesus' prayer for His people, "That they be one as He and the Father are one." God will judge those who divide the flock.

Unity cannot be legislated. Unity is a conscious belonging of one part with the whole. As the body has been used in illustration, all the parts of the body are one body. When one member of the body is injured, the whole body aches together with it. When the injured member is healed, the whole body rejoices with it. So it is with the family of God. There is a belonging to the body of Christ by virtue of the new birth. When we are born into the family of God, we belong to God and are *in* the family. We belong. There is a great swelling love that reaches out and embraces all those of kindred spirit. Unity occurs because God implants us (branches) into Jesus (the vine) and we all become one, bearing the fruit of the gospel. Any man, organization, or group that presumes to declare who is in and who is out is on a path that will collide with the wrath of Almighty God. One member of the body cannot simply declare another member to be "not" of the body. Men do not set the members into the Body of Christ; God sets the members.

Thank God our salvation is not dependent on man's opinions. God knows the heart and can rightly judge the hearts of His people. Man's judgment will fail every time.

Notice Paul's admonition:

> "Finally, brethren, farewell. Be perfect, be of good comfort, be of one mind, live in peace; and the God of love and peace shall be with you" (2 Corinthians 13:11).

> "Endeavouring to keep the unity of the Spirit in the bond of peace" (Ephesians 4:3).

> "Finally, be ye all of one mind, having compassion one of another, love as brethren, be pitiful, be courteous" (1 Peter 3:8).

> "Neither pray I for these alone, but for them also which shall believe on me through their word; That they all may be one; as thou, Father, art in me, and I in thee, that they

also may be one in us: that the world may believe that thou hast sent me" (John 17:20-21).

If God is in the heart of Christ and Christ is in the heart of the believer, then all believers are in kinship with one another and with God the Father and the Son Jesus Christ. We are family.

CHAPTER TEN

The Antichrist

The concept of the antichrist is one of the most misunderstood doctrines in the Bible. A vast majority of the denominations have accepted the teaching that in the days just before the return of Christ a great deceiver will arise and sweep the world with his charms. Then he will show himself to be the great evil one leading the world into rebellion against Christ in that last final spiritual battle called Armageddon. It is believed that this religious superman will establish the great counterfeit religious system that will carry most Christians away in its deceptions. Although teachers of this doctrine refer to other scripture to support their teaching, there are only four scriptures that refer to the term *antichrist*. One such verse is 2 Thessalonians 2:3-4, which says, "Let no man deceive you by any means: for that day shall not come, except there come a falling away first, and that man of sin be revealed, the son of perdition; Who opposeth and exalteth himself above all that is called God, or that is worshipped; so that he as God sitteth in the temple of God, shewing himself that he is God." This is speaking of the "man of sin" that must be revealed, the "son of perdition." This verse has no application to any of the verses referring to "the" antichrist and is treated in its proper place in the chapter discussing the millennium.

> "Little children, it is the last time: and as ye have heard that antichrist shall come, even now are there many antichrists; whereby we know that it is the last time" (1 John 2:18).

Note that John begins this verse saying, "it is the last time." He is not referring to the end of the world, but to the time in which he was living "*it is*" the last time. He then reminds them that they have been warned that "antichrist" should come. He then indicates that there are "many" antichrists already in the world. Not one, but many. He uses the fact that "many" antichrists are already in the world as validation that he considered his own day to be the beginning of the last days. Or as he put it, the "last time."

> "Who is a liar but he that denieth that Jesus is the Christ? He is antichrist, that denieth the Father and the Son" (1 John 2:22).

Here, John begins to identify who this antichrist is. Religious liars or deceivers are antichrist. We have religions that do not believe that Jesus is truly of miraculous birth or that He rose bodily from the grave and ascended to heaven. Others, though religious and having some sort of worship, do not even believe that God is a real person, but more of a concept of personal good. Others believe that all material things are god. You, me, animals, trees, all living things are part of that which makes up what we call God. John is making it clear that anyone who denies that Jesus is the Messiah, and that God is the great creator, the eternal, the living God, is antichrist. That is, they are "against" Christ. Basically then, antichrist is anyone criticizing, ridiculing, or deriding the name of Christ. At the present time here in America, there is a great political crisis over the use of the name of God and the name of Christ. Those who have fought against Christianity over the last fifty years have induced our political leaders to ban the use of the names God and Christ, and the use of religious slogans, placards or banners, and prayers in schools, courthouses, and many other places. This is exactly what John was talking about. Again, *anti* means to be against something or someone. Our generation is denying and rejecting Christ. In this light, many of our political leaders today are antichrist.

First John 4:3 says, "And every spirit that confesseth not that Jesus Christ is come in the flesh is not of God: and this is that spirit of antichrist, whereof ye have heard that it should come; and even now already is it in the world."

In the above scripture, John tells us that anyone who does not acknowledge Jesus as God incarnate, who was born of a virgin, lived as a man, died, and rose from the dead is antichrist. John also says that this is a spiritual condition. Man has a nature "spirit" within him that is good, bad, or indifferent, that believes or disbelieves. That nature is the spirit within him. Those who will not acknowledge the deity of Christ have a spirit of antichrist. John once again affirms that this spirit against Christ is already in the world. Such ungodly opposers of Christ were among them in that day, and that same spirit is among us today: "For *many deceivers* are entered into the world, who confess not that Jesus Christ is come in the flesh. This is a deceiver and an antichrist" (2 John 7).

This text simply reiterates what has been said before and need not be enlarged upon at this point. John is saying that in his own day, many deceivers, liars, and deniers of Christ are in the world. They are anti-against-Christ.

In the above scriptures, John clearly identifies antichrist as a spirit or nature that is hostile to Christ and that there were many in the world already in his day, as there are many in our time also. In no place does he use the definite article to describe the term as a single person as the modern teaching does—that is, as "the antichrist." At no time does the apostle insinuate that a particular person would become the great opposer of Christ, nor does he indicate that at some future date, such a one would appear. The King James or Authorized Version of the Bible has been the accepted authority of God's Word for four hundred years. This version of the Bible uses the indefinite article to describe antichrist (*an* antichrist), never the definite article (the antichrist). Use of the definite article became common in translations made in recent times. Modern translations validate their revisions by claiming that they are more up to date and readable. The truth of the matter is that most modern translations diminish the power of the Blood of the Lord Jesus Christ by altering and in many cased actually removing scriptures contained in the Authorized Version of the Bible.

CHAPTER ELEVEN

Armageddon

As a child, I was told the story of a coming battle of Armageddon, a great battle between the good people and the bad people in which the blood of mankind would run through the streets and be as deep as a horse's bridle. I feared and dreaded this event because I was very small and not as tall as a horse's bridle, and I thought I would surely drown in all that blood. When we take prophetic symbolic language and try to literalize it, all kinds of confusing images are possible.

In brief, the doctrine of Armageddon is presented as the final battle of this age in which God intervenes to destroy the armies of Satan and to cast Satan into the lake of fire. Scholars disagree about the exact location of this great battle, but the most likely possibility is the valley between Mount Carmel and Mount Gilboa. This valley, known as the Valley of Jezreel and sometimes referred to as the Plain of Esdraelon, was the crossroads of two ancient trade routes and thus was a strategic military site. *Armageddon* is the Greek word for this area, which was the scene of many ancient battles. Scripturally, Megiddo has become the symbolic battleground for the final conflict or war between the forces of good and the forces of evil.

The only mention of Armageddon is in Revelation 16:12-16, which says, "And the sixth angel poured out his vial upon the great river Euphrates; and the water thereof was dried up, that the way of the kings of the east might be prepared. And I saw three unclean spirits like frogs come out of the mouth of the dragon, and out of the mouth of the beast, and out of the mouth of the false prophet. For they are the spirits of devils, working miracles, which go forth unto the kings of the earth and of the whole world, to gather them to the battle of that great day of God Almighty. Behold, I come as a thief. Blessed is he that watcheth, and keepeth his garments, lest he walk naked, and they see his shame. And he gathered them together into a place called in the Hebrew tongue Armageddon."

Note the message of the revelation.

1. It is a "revealing" from God through Christ.
2. It is a message to His servants, the redeemed. Not to the world.
3. Things must "shortly come to pass."

"The Revelation of Jesus Christ, which God gave unto him, to shew unto his servants things which must shortly come to pass; and he sent and signified it by his angel unto his servant John" (Revelation 1:1).

The reason that there are so many interpretations of the book of Revelation is that men are trying to analyze it in a literal sense, which cannot be done by the scholarly application of educated translation. It is a spiritual message about spiritual things to a spiritual people who understand by "revelation" of God and not human wisdom.

Since it is a message to the church and not the world, it is in language understood by the church but confusing to the world. Remember that Jesus spoke in parables that His disciples but not the unbelievers might understand His words.

Matthew 13:10-11 says, "And the disciples came, and said unto him, Why speakest thou unto them in parables? He answered and said unto them, Because it is given unto you to know the *mysteries* of the kingdom of heaven, but to them it is not given."

To properly identify Armageddon, we must interpret the scripture that refers to it. The very first thing we see, and the most important, is the time line as it fits into the Bible's chronology. First of all, the study of the revelation is a spiritual message to the church of the gospel dispensation, the period between the beginning of the church age to the end of time. Armageddon is a part of the message of the sixth angel. There are seven angels having seven trumpets. Each angel blows his trumpet or sounds his message to one of the seven churches. These churches are not the literal churches named in Asia, but the Church of God of the New Testament and each of the angels are speaking to the church during different periods of the gospel day. Remember, Jesus built only "one" church. Since the battle of Armageddon is part of the message to the church by the sixth angel and not the seventh, Armageddon cannot be applied only to the end of the world. We do not have space or time to discourse on the interpretation of the book of Revelation, but we will try to give the application for this verse. The vital elements of Revelation 16:12-16 are as follows:

1. Vial — The judgments of God
2. Euphrates — Water is people and Euphrates is Babylon or sectarian religions.
3. Frogs — Filthy communication (doctrine) out of the mouth of the dragon, beast, and false prophet
4. Dragon — Satanic opposition to God and His Church (pagan persecution)
5. Beast — Counterfeit church set up by the dragon (Catholicism)
6. False prophet — Corrupt religious leaders (sectarianism)
7. Garments — Spiritual garb, robes of righteousness, or unrighteous filthy rags
8. Nakedness — Spiritual condition of the unsaved (Robe of righteousness is missing.)

We see here a time when God is pouring out judgment (*vials*) on the enemies of God. It is the sixth angel pouring out his vial (judgments) on the river Euphrates (sectarianism). When a faithful ministry preaches the pure Word of God, judgment is pronounced on the disobedient. In the time line of the gospel day, we see this sixth angel prophesying in the latter half of the nineteenth century and into the twentieth century. From ancient times, Satan has opposed God. Satan opposed Jesus during His life's ministry, and he has opposed the church from its beginning and continues to do so to this day. Satan opposed the early days of the church by persecution. He stirred up the Romans to wage general persecutions, through the great red dragon (Revelation 12:1-3). Failing to destroy the church by elimination, he tried by counterfeiting the church and the Church of Rome evolved, the *beast* (Revelation 13:1-5), which tried to replace the spiritual with the ritual (idolatry). The sixteenth-century Reformation proved that these tactics had failed and Satan then made an "image" of the beast (Revelation 13:14-15), producing the *false prophet*, sectarianism. Each of these corrupt religious systems attempted to mislead God's people by doctrinal confusion. One of the principal admonitions of the apostles was that they all speak the same thing, as it says in First Corinthians: "Now I beseech you, brethren, by the name of our Lord Jesus Christ, that ye all speak the same thing, and that there be no divisions among you; but that ye be perfectly joined together" (1 Corinthians 1:10).

Consider all the denominations of religion available today. You can literally believe anything and find a church that will support it, no matter how ridiculous it might be. The farther we go in time, the more the world is coming into the churches filling them with all kinds of corrupt doctrine, "unclean spirits like frogs." Doctrines are coming out of the mouth of the false religious systems such as paganism, Catholicism, and the false prophet, which is the ministry of the modern sectarian systems. One church tells you there is a God; the next says there is not. Another tells you that you cannot live without sinning more or less, yet God's Word declares that "sin is of the devil" (1 John 3:8). Another ordains homosexuals into the ministry, yet God made homosexuality a capital offense. Another teaches that once you are saved, you cannot be lost, yet the apostle Paul recognized that if he failed to remain faithful, he himself might become a castaway (1 Corinthians 9:27). Another teaches that God has predetermined who will be saved and who will not, which is known as "predestination." Yet God says that "whosoever will" may be saved (Revelation 22:17), "it is not the will of God that any should perish" (2 Peter 3:9). As you can see, you can find a religion that will teach anything you want. A young woman once declared, "I am going to visit as many churches as necessary until I find one that teaches what I believe." All of this confusion is Satan's method of misleading souls and dragging them down into a devil's hell.

When the Bible talks about blood as it does in the case of Armageddon, it is referring to the blood of souls. With so many denominations teaching so many different doctrines and many of them being devoid of a genuine experience of soul-saving grace, millions of religious people trust a delusion that will ultimately land them in hell. These lost souls are the blood of Armageddon. Blood flowing as deep as the horse's bridle is simply a way to describe the horrible magnitude of lost souls believing themselves to be right even though they are still lost. The battle has been raging since the beginning, but in these last days, Satan has mustered all his cohorts and is waging the hottest battle ever. He is working through not only church deception, but through governments as well, trying to eliminate God's influence upon men. We also see in these perilous times an enemy attacking head-on. The Muslim empire is attacking Christianity and is using our own government and laws to do so. Armageddon is a spiritual battle that is raging in this present day and is intensifying as time grows toward the end. The reason for using the term *Armageddon* is that in ancient times, Armageddon, or the valley of Megiddo, was the crossroads of the Middle East. Whoever controlled this area controlled all commerce from Africa to Persia. Megiddo was a fortified city guarding the pass of Megiddo, through which not only commerce, but also armies passed. It also was the primary site for many of the battles of ancient times. When King Saul went to fight the Philistines, it was at Mount Gilboa, the eastern border of the valley. The battle of Armageddon is in full array today. The battle is raging now, and the blood of souls truly is flowing like a river.

CHAPTER TWELVE

Eternal Security

The final habitation of the soul after death is of great importance. Most people believe in a heaven or a hell. We believe that there is a life after death and that there will be a general judgment before the throne of God when this life is over. The penalty for sin is eternal damnation; the benefit of righteousness is eternal life. The verdict at that judgment will be final, and there will be no appeal. Therefore, it is sound practice to prepare our case in advance, to "make our calling and election sure."

Second Peter 1:10 says, "Wherefore the rather, brethren, give diligence to make your calling and election sure: for if ye do these things, ye shall never fall."

Many people in this age of religious confusion and misunderstanding declare themselves to be "born again" or "saved by the Blood of Jesus" while living a life far below the principles outlined in the Word of God. Corruption, compromise, and deceit are pouring forth from many pulpits across the land, and countless souls are being consigned to eternal death and damnation because they have believed a lie and consequently are not prepared to meet an angry God at the judgment. Therefore, it behooves every professing Christian to look to his own spiritual well-being. He cannot simply "trust" the modern pastor. There is a truth or a right way of life, and that truth is found in the Bible, the Word of God. Failing to ascertain the truth from God's Word and following human wisdom will result in eternal loss of the soul.

"And then shall that Wicked be revealed, whom the Lord shall consume with the spirit of his mouth, and shall destroy with the brightness of his coming: Even him, whose coming is after the working of Satan with all power and signs and lying wonders, And with all deceivableness of unrighteousness in them that perish; because they received not the love of the truth, that they might be saved. And for this cause God shall send them strong delusion, that they should believe a lie: That they all might be damned who believed not the truth, but had pleasure in unrighteousness" (2 Thessalonians 2:8-12).

We all hold the apostles of Jesus in high regard. They are, by the inspiration of God, the authors of the New Testament. However, those who heard them did not simply swallow everything they spoke; *they checked it out*, as it says in Acts 17:11: "These were more noble than those in Thessalonica, in that they received the word with all readiness of mind, and *searched the scriptures daily, whether those things were so.*"

Although our pastors will be held to account for the souls that have been lost for their lack of care, we also stand responsible for our own soul, as we have the full Word of God at our disposal and can prove the truth or lie of what is being preached to us. God will not accept our plea "my pastor said." Salvation is a personal experience, and we accept the terms of Jesus and live accordingly, or we believe the lies or deceit being promulgated today and perish.

One facet of this doctrine believes that one cannot avoid sin while in this life: "Every man sins daily in thought, word, and deed." I visited in the home of a family who were members of a denominational church. At every table grace, the words *forgive us of our sins* were included. A fundamental doctrine of their church is that the believer cannot avoid sin in thought, word, and deed. They teach that in the human, sin is unavoidable, and therefore you must constantly seek forgiveness of your sins of the day. The question that jumps up in my mind is, What will happen if the Lord comes while I am committing one of those sins? We could run through the "what-ifs" all day, but let's settle the question of sin. Let us identify what sin is. Sin is disobedience to God, the transgression of God's Word, as we read in First John: "Whosoever committeth sin transgresseth also the law: for sin is the transgression of the law" (1 John 3:4).

Here we see that sin is the violation of the law or God's commandments. Whether we realize it or not, we are under the sovereign rule and authority of God, and our eternal security is based solely on how we honor His commandments. If we do what the Word of God commands us to do not, we sin and fall under the condemnation of eternal death. If we don't do what the Word of God says to do, we fall under the sin of omission and stand guilty before God. Sin is any disobedience toward God or His Word. The basic commandments instruct us to love God and our brother (fellow man), to keep the Sabbath or a day of worship, and to honor our father and mother. We are commanded not to steal, kill, commit adultery, bear false witness, covet, lust, cheat, lie, hate, and deceive, and the list could go on and on. When we fail on any of those things, we fail the test of obedience and fall under guilt, and yet we are told to *sin not*.

First John 3:5-10 says, "And ye know that he was manifested to take away our sins; and in him is no sin. Whosoever abideth in him sinneth not: whosoever sinneth hath not seen him, neither known him. Little children, let no man deceive you: he that doeth righteousness is righteous, even as he is righteous. He that committeth sin is of the devil; for the devil sinneth from the beginning. For this purpose the Son of God was manifested, that he might destroy the works of the devil. Whosoever is born of God doth not commit sin; for his seed remaineth in him: and he cannot sin, because he is born of God. In this the children of God are manifest, and the children of the devil: whosoever doeth not righteousness is not of God, neither he that loveth not his brother."

Notice in the scripture above that Jesus came to *take away* our sins, not to save us *in* our sins. Those who abide in Jesus "sinneth not." Those that commit sin "hath not seen him, neither known him." God has offered no tolerance for sin, and all sin is ascribed to the Devil. "He that committeth sin is of the devil; for the devil sinneth from the beginning." Jesus' purpose in coming and dying on the cross was for our salvation and the destruction of the works of the Devil (*sin*). "For this purpose the Son of God was manifested, that he might destroy the works of the devil" (1 John 3:8).

Jesus told Nicodemus that he must be "born again." We hear many testify today that they are "born-again Christians," yet their lives bear sinful stains. Dear reader, please comprehend that any sin in your life precludes you from being "born again" and you are still in your sins. A person who is "born again" *does not commit sin*. "Whosoever is born of God doth not commit sin; for his seed remaineth in him: and he cannot sin, because he is born of God" (1 John 3:9). This scripture makes it clear that a child of God *does not sin*.

Another facet of this doctrine is that "once in grace, always in grace." Some of our denominations believe that the Blood of Christ covers all sin, past, present, and future. It is believed that once you are saved, your salvation cannot be lost even when you sin in the future. They believe that even future sins are covered by the Blood and that you are eternally secure. This damnable doctrine is a formula for consigning souls in advance to destruction. Depending on this concept of eternal security, many will permit themselves to be frivolous in their speech and actions. I once knew a man who was a prominent member of a church that practiced this doctrine. This man worked as a mechanic and so was ideal to maintain the church bus. He also drove the church bus to pick up children for Sunday School. This man used filthy language. He could curse, swear, and use the name of God and Jesus Christ in the most derogatory fashion. As a violator of the commandment not to take the name of God in vain, this man was glaringly guilty of *sin,* yet he was a member in good standing. He believed the Blood covered his present sins as well as those he was going to commit tomorrow. A woman asked me one time what I thought about the doctrine of eternal security. I explained to her that all sin must be forever forsaken and any sin committed made us guilty before God and subject to eternal damnation. She responded, "Oh, I couldn't make it without it" (the doctrine of the eternal security). What this woman did not comprehend is that she could not make it with it.

If the doctrine of eternal security were true, it would suggest that it is impossible for a man to backslide after once giving his heart to the Lord. A man might say, "I was saved forty years ago at an altar of prayer in a little chapel on any street in Some Town, California." I would have no reason to doubt the truth of his witness to salvation. I can believe he truly was saved from sin forty years ago. But how has he lived from that time till today? Has this man remained sinless? Or has he trusted eternal security to take him through despite his returning to sin? The question we need to answer is, can a man backslide? Can we find any scriptural evidence that a man approved of God could turn away from God and not be held under God's judgment? Or will God punish a righteous man after he turns to unrighteousness?

To begin with, let's look back to the Garden of Eden. Adam was created in righteousness but expelled from the garden in unrighteousness because of sin. When God delivered Israel out of Egypt, the people were saved from bondage of servitude, like Christians are saved from the bondage of sin. Yet, among this "saved" assembly of Israel was one disobedient man, Achan, who when discovered was taken out with all he had, including family, and slain and buried. He paid the penalty for his disobedience to the commandment of God (Joshua 7:19-26). Solomon, one of the greatest kings in Bible history, was honored by God with wisdom, power, and rule. His kingdom spread from the Mediterranean Sea to the Euphrates River. Yet in his old age he forsook the commandments of God, turning to idolatry, and lost his honor and kingdom . . . Israel in their disobedience was delivered into the hands of the king of Babylon and again was placed into bondage and servitude. Throughout Old Testament history after God gave sufficient warning to His people, He executed judgment on them for their violation of His Word.

Paul in his letter to the Romans drew an illustration of ancient Israel during their passage through the wilderness while traveling from Egypt to Canaan. When God led Israel to the border of Canaan, desiring them to enter the land and take possession of it, the people refused, and God declared judgment on that generation, condemning them to die in the wilderness. The point that Paul is making here is that if God brought judgment on that generation for disobedience, what makes us think He will spare us, who now have more perfect knowledge, when we violate the commands of God?

Romans 11:21-22 says, "For if God spared not the natural branches, take heed lest he also spare not thee. Behold therefore the goodness and severity of God: on them which fell (*sinned*) severity; but toward thee, goodness, if thou continue in his goodness: otherwise thou also shalt be cut off.

New Testament doctrine declares that our security is in obedience to the Word of God. Therefore, if we honor God's Word in obedience, God's goodness on our lives is promised. On the other hand, if we fail to "continue" in our walk of obedience, "severity" is the rule. Paul is speaking to Christian Gentiles and is telling these "saved" Gentiles that if they do not continue in their Christian walk, they also will be "cut off," as it was with ancient Israel when they failed to continue following God.

Read 1 Corinthians 9:27 and 1 Corinthians 10:1-12.

In the verses in First Corinthians, Paul is again referring to Israel in their sojourn in the wilderness. Paul is reinforcing the point that God did not withhold judgment on old Israel and He will not withhold judgment on us if we return to sin.

"But I keep under my body, and bring it into subjection: lest that by any means, when I have preached to others, I myself should be a castaway" (1 Corinthians 9:27). Paul in this verse is referring to himself. I believe we all hold Paul the apostle to be a saved and anointed servant of God who is looking forward to the "crown of life" set before him. Paul here declares that he daily keeps watch over his own actions and behavior, acknowledging that should he fail in his pursuit of the gospel, he also could become a castaway. Whatever happened to eternal security? If Paul was saved, how could he ever be a castaway? As we can see, the Bible does not overlook sin in anybody. Even after a man bows at an altar of prayer, accepting the atonement of Christ's Blood, he falls under the judgment of God and will pay the price if he sins.

Ezekiel 3:20 says, "Again, When a righteous man doth turn from his righteousness, and commit iniquity, and I lay a stumbling block before him, he shall die: because thou hast not given him warning, *he shall die in his sin, and his righteousness which he hath done shall not be remembered*; but his blood will I require at thine hand."

In the above scripture, Ezekiel is making it clear that a righteous man who turns from his righteousness will die *in* his sin and his righteousness will not be remembered. My friends, nowhere in the scriptures are we told that we can sin after becoming saved and still retain our salvation. On the other hand we are told time and again that if we sin, the wrath of God will abide on us.

Do not be deceived. Note the following verses:

> "And ye shall be hated of all men for my name's sake: but he that endureth to the end shall be saved" (Matthew 10:22).

> "But Christ as a son over his own house; whose house are we, if we hold fast the confidence and the rejoicing of the hope firm unto the end" (Hebrews 3:6).

> "For we are made partakers of Christ, if we hold the beginning of our confidence stedfast unto the end" (Hebrews 3:14).

The Christian walk is one of loyalty to God and His Word. We will love and honor the object of our affection. Loving God means doing as Jesus did.

> "And he that sent me is with me: the Father hath not left me alone; for I do always those things that please him" (John 8:29).

If we commit ourselves to "always pleasing Him," there will be no sin to break our relationship with Him. If we sin, it is because we love ourselves more than we love God, which in itself is a breaking of the commandment to love God with all our heart, mind, and soul. Let us not risk our eternal soul on doctrines of men that cannot be validated by the Bible. Check it out, and do your due diligence; search the scriptures daily to see if those things they teach you are so. Eternity is too long and life is too short to risk being wrong.

One final point: The apostle John when identifying the seriousness of sin did not make any allowances for continuing in sin after becoming saved. The apostle's attitude is laid out in the following scriptures:

> "Whosoever committeth sin transgresseth also the law: for sin is the transgression of the law. And ye know that he was manifested to take away our sins; and in him is no sin" (1 John 3:4-5).

> "He that committeth sin is of the devil; for the devil sinneth from the beginning. For this purpose the Son of God was manifested, that he might destroy the works of the devil. Whosoever is born of God doth not commit sin; for his seed remaineth in him: and he cannot sin, because he is born of God." (1 John 3:8-9).

CHAPTER THIRTEEN

Homosexuality

One of the most heartbreaking trends flowing through our religious world today is the movement toward homosexuality in our churches. Not only the religious world, but also general society traditionally has shunned homosexuality. However, from time to time throughout this world's history, those giving themselves to such practices "come out of the closet" and demand their rights to free expression of their sexual orientation. Such demand for free expression has moved from the public arena into the churches. The question many of our mainline denominations are faced with today is, Do we accept homosexuals as members in good standing in the church? And do we ordain them into the ministry and put them in the pulpits? Sexuality is not simply a physical act between two people. It is also a spiritual act and must be performed in that context. When God created humankind, He created them male and female. God brought them together and commanded them to be fruitful, and to reproduce.

Genesis 1:28 says, "And God blessed them, and God said unto them, Be fruitful, and multiply, and replenish the earth, and subdue it: and have dominion over the fish of the sea, and over the fowl of the air, and over every living thing that moveth upon the earth."

The apostle Paul shows us that the sexual relationship between a husband and wife is a matter of one's right to the other and that one may not withhold himself from his spouse without reason. All sins committed by a person are between that person and God. All sexual sins are a violation of the defrauded spouse. Sexual activity is designed by God to be engaged in by a husband and wife.

> "Marriage is honourable in all, and the bed undefiled: but whoremongers and adulterers God will judge. The wife hath not power of her own body, but the husband: and likewise also the husband hath not power of his own body, but the wife. Defraud ye not one the other, except it be with consent for a time, that ye may give yourselves to fasting and prayer; and come together again, that Satan tempt you not for your incontinency" (Hebrews 13:4-5).

The wife has a duty to surrender her body to her husband, and the husband has a duty to surrender his body to his wife unless they together choose to abstain for some purpose. The body of the wife is not hers to give to another nor is the body of the man. The body of the husband belongs to the wife and the body of the wife belongs to the husband, and to give that body to another is a most serious violation of trust. God likens our relationship with Him as a relationship between a husband and wife. See for instance, the following passage from Ephesians: "For we are members of his body, of his flesh, and of his bones. For this cause shall a man leave his father and mother, and shall be joined unto his wife, and they two shall be one flesh. This is a great mystery: but I speak concerning Christ and the church" (Ephesians 5:30-32).

Some time ago, I read an article in the *Press Telegram* newspaper published in Long Beach, California, where a religious leader declared that the Bible has no clear denunciation of homosexual practice. The truth is there are sixteen passages directly dealing with homosexuality. In many of the references, it is God doing the talking. Let me refer to a few.

> "Do not lie with a man as one lies with a woman; that is detestable. Do not have sexual relations with an animal and defile yourself with it. A woman must not present

herself to an animal to have sexual relations with it; that is a perversion" (Leviticus 18:22-23, NIV).

"If a man lies with a man as one lies with a woman, both of them have done what is detestable. They must be put to death; their blood will be on their own heads" (Leviticus 20:13, NIV).

"There shall be no whore of the daughters of Israel, nor a sodomite of the sons of Israel" (Deuteronomy 23:17, KJV).

These are direct instructions from God Himself as He was giving forth the law of Moses. God's response to the unnatural use of sexual activity is death. It was a capital offense. God did not create man nor intend for man to satisfy his lust with another man. Neither was a woman intended to satisfy her lust with another woman. Nor was a person to satisfy their lust by engaging in sexual practices with an animal. The city of Sodom was destroyed because of the practice of "sodomy" (homosexuality) among all the population. God anointed the sexual union between a man and his wife for the purpose of personal intimacy and procreation. Such cannot be accomplished between people of the same sex.

The scriptures are not limited to the Old Testament. Note the following:

"Therefore God gave them over in the sinful desires of their hearts to sexual impurity for the degrading of their bodies with one another" (Romans 1:24, NIV).

"Because of this, God gave them over to shameful lusts. Even their women exchanged natural relations for unnatural ones. In the same way the men also abandoned natural relations with women and were inflamed with lust for one another. Men committed indecent acts with other men, and received in themselves the due penalty for their perversion" (Romans 1:26-27, NIV).

"Do you not know that the wicked will not inherit the
kingdom of God? do not be deceived: Neither the sexually
immoral nor idolaters nor adulterers nor male prostitutes
nor homosexual offenders" (1 Corinthians 6:9, NIV).

As you can see, the Bible has a great deal to say about homosexuality,
both in the Old Testament and in the New. Our laws are designed to
preserve the peace, not dictate morality. Therefore, those who choose
the "alternate lifestyle" are at liberty to do so under the protection of
the law. But such practice is in violation of God's law, which cannot be
successfully disputed. Those of us who choose to be governed by God's
law cannot and will not sanction homosexuality. We don't take such a
position simply to be against homosexuality, but because transgressing
God's law brings damnation to the soul. Many of our "gays" are seeking
religious acceptance, and many of our denominations are reworking
their standards to accommodate them. What all these people are
forgetting is that God's laws are immutable. "I am the Lord, I change
not" (Malachi 3:6). "Sin is the transgression of the law" (1 John 3:4).
"The wages of sin is death" (Romans 6:23).

No man can alter the Word of God. Practices that came under the curse
of death four thousand years ago, two thousand years ago, are under
the same penalty today. Although you have a right to exercise your
attitudes and opinions on this matter, God's Word and His judgments
do not change. You alone must deal with any consequences. You alone
must explain yourself to God.

CHAPTER FOURTEEN

Lucifer

A Fallen Angel?

Note: This chapter requires a different approach for its exposition. It is a saga of God interacting with men and nations. Much of the dialogue comes from Isaiah's prophecies and Daniel's dreams and visions. In this chapter nearly all of the thirteenth and fourteenth chapters of Isaiah are included. It is important that the reader read all the scripture presented in order to follow the course of events.

How many times have we heard Satan referred to as Lucifer? How many times have we seen a hideous image of a beast with horns, tail, and pitchfork identified as Lucifer? We are going to deal with the subject of Satan as a fallen angel, quoting scriptures in Isaiah 14, Ezekiel 28, and Luke 10. Let's approach the subject as God suggests, with some common reasoning.

Isaiah 1:18 says, "Come now, and let us reason together, saith the Lord."

Considering whether Satan was ever in heaven, we need to ask how and when he appeared on the human scene. Is he human, spirit, or angel? Was he before the beginning or did he appear sometime in later history? We know that angels, cherubim, seraphim, and so on as well as humankind are all created beings. We also know that humankind was created differently from any other of God's creation because God infused his Spirit into the man and "he became a living soul." As a living soul we receive a "moral" nature. We can choose to obey God or we can choose to sin. The angels are spirits in themselves, and there is no scriptural evidence that true angels possessed the will to sin.

Consider this. If Satan was an angel of God who rebelled and was cast out, what would prevent another angel from doing the same thing? What if another angel rebelled and prevailed against God and our heaven was ruled by a tyrannical angel? Where would we get our security of eternal bliss? Who would choose a heaven if its future were uncertain?

Before considering the scriptures that teachers of this doctrine use to prove that Satan was cast out of heaven, we will start by citing the leading verse of several important messages that God was transmitting through Isaiah. You will notice that each prophetic message begins with "The burden of." A few other definitions of the word burden are "problem," "load," and "affliction."

> "**The burden of Babylon**, which Isaiah the son of Amoz did see" (Isaiah 13:1).

> "**The burden of Moab**. Because in the night Ar of Moab is laid waste, and brought to silence; because in the night Kir of Moab is laid waste, and brought to silence" (Isaiah 15:1).

> "**The burden of** Damascus. Behold, Damascus is taken away from being a city, and it shall be a ruinous heap" (Isaiah 17:1).

> "**The burden of Egypt.** Behold, the Lord rideth upon a swift cloud, and shall come into Egypt: and the idols of Egypt shall be moved at his presence, and the heart of Egypt shall melt in the midst of it" (Isaiah 19:1).

"**The burden of Tyre**. Howl, ye ships of Tarshish; for it is laid waste, so that there is no house, no entering in: from the land of Chittim it is revealed to them" (Isaiah 23:1).

To deal with the subject of Isaiah 14 we must go back to chapter 13 to find out what the burden or message is about. In this case the subject of the prophecy was Babylon. Since Lucifer appears in this segment of prophecy, he must belong to the time of this prophecy and the judgments must also be pertinent to this time. Prophecy does not reach rearward; it reaches forward. Therefore, Lucifer of Isaiah cannot be the serpent of Genesis. If Lucifer is not the serpent of Genesis, neither can he be Satan. Also consider that this prophecy came by the prophet Isaiah, who prophesied from 762 BC to 698 BC. Furthermore the prophecy specifically was given in the year that King Ahaz died, 724 BC. (Notice verse 28 of Isaiah 14.) If Satan were cast out of heaven by the judgments of this prophecy, then there would have been no devil before this time.

Nebuchadnezzar, the king of Babylon, was actually a tool in the hand of the Lord for the punishing of the two southern tribes of Judah. Historically, Babylon as a world power appears only for a short time. God sends Jeremiah to instruct the Jews to surrender to Nebuchadnezzar, whom God refers to as "my servant" (Jeremiah 27:6; 25:9). Judah is thus to be punished for seventy years (Jeremiah 25:11-12). Had Judah obeyed the Lord and surrendered to Nebuchadnezzar, Jerusalem and Solomon's temple would not have been destroyed. God struggled with Judah for so long that they passed the point of no return. God's mercy was no longer open to them, and only judgment was their future.

"But they mocked the messengers of God, and despised his words, and misused his prophets, *until the wrath of the Lord arose against his people, till there was no remedy.* Therefore he brought upon them the king of the Chaldees, who slew their young men with the sword in the house of their sanctuary, and had no compassion upon young man or maiden, old man, or him that stooped for age: he gave them all into his hand" (2 Chronicles 36:16-17).

Once the limit of God's patience and mercy are exceeded, there is no other means of salvation. The Jews, had passed the point of "no return." There was **no remedy**. Judgment was declared and certain.

Listen to Jeremiah

"In the beginning of the reign of Jehoiakim the son of Josiah king of Judah came this word unto Jeremiah from the Lord, saying, Thus saith the Lord to me; Make thee bonds and yokes, and put them upon thy neck, And send them to the king of Edom, and to the king of Moab, and to the king of the Ammonites, and to the king of Tyrus, and to the king of Zidon, by the hand of the messengers which come to Jerusalem unto Zedekiah king of Judah; And command them to say unto their masters, Thus saith the Lord of hosts, the God of Israel; Thus shall ye say unto your masters; I have made the earth, the man and the beast that are upon the ground, by my great power and by my outstretched arm, and have given it unto whom it seemed meet unto me. And now have I given all these lands unto the hand of Nebuchadnezzar the king of Babylon, my servant; and the beasts of the field have I given him also to serve him. And all nations shall serve him, and his son, and his son's son, until the very time of his land come: and then many nations and great kings shall serve themselves of him. And it shall come to pass, that the nation and kingdom which will not serve the same Nebuchadnezzar the king of Babylon, and that will not put their neck under the yoke of the king of Babylon, that nation will I punish, saith the Lord, with the sword, and with the famine, and with the pestilence, until I have consumed them by his hand. Therefore hearken not ye to your prophets, nor to your diviners, nor to your dreamers, nor to your enchanters, nor to your sorcerers, which speak unto you, saying, Ye shall not serve the king of Babylon: For they prophesy a lie unto you, to remove you far from your land; and that I should drive you out, and ye should perish. But the nations that bring their neck under the yoke of the king of Babylon, and serve him, those will I let remain still in their own land, saith the Lord; and they shall till it, and dwell therein." (Jeremiah 27:1-11)

Once judgment had been pronounced, God made it clear that the nations that came from Abraham's seed will be ruled by Nebuchadnezzar, king of Babylon. However, if the Jews would surrender and bow to the yoke of the king of Babylon, their lands, cities, and temple would not be destroyed and they would be allowed to live in peace in their own land. If they refused and fought the king of Babylon, then they and their lands, cities, and temple would be destroyed. And so it was.

"For thus saith the Lord of hosts, the God of Israel; I have put a yoke of iron upon the neck of all these nations, that they may serve Nebuchadnezzar king of Babylon; and they shall serve him: and I have given him the beasts of the field also" (Jeremiah 28:12).

"Behold, I will send and take all the families of the north, saith the Lord, and Nebuchadnezzar the king of Babylon, my servant, and will bring them against this land, and against the inhabitants thereof, and against all these nations round about, and will utterly destroy them, and make them an astonishment, and an hissing, and perpetual desolations. Moreover I will take from them the voice of mirth, and the voice of gladness, the voice of the bridegroom, and the voice of the bride, the sound of the millstones, and the light of the candle. And this whole land shall be a desolation, and an astonishment; and these nations shall serve the king of Babylon seventy years. And it shall come to pass, when seventy years are accomplished, that I will punish the king of Babylon, and that nation, saith the Lord, for their iniquity, and the land of the Chaldeans, and will make it perpetual desolations. And I will bring upon that land all my words which I have pronounced against it, even all that is written in this book, which Jeremiah hath prophesied against all the nations." (Jeremiah 25:9-13)

Nebuchadnezzar's army did besiege Jerusalem, carried most of the population away, and scattered them throughout the provinces of Babylon in the year 606 BC. They remained in captivity for the seventy years as prophesied and were released to return by Cyrus, the king of Persia, in 536 BC. By this time, Babylon as a world power was no more, and the judgment against it remains to this day.

Note: Various Bible scholars differ on the dates concerning the seventy years. Nebuchadnezzar made several campaigns into the land of Canaan. Individual opinion on the date will depend on which invasion campaign is used as a starting point.

Let's look into Isaiah's prophecy!

First of all, chapters 13 and 14 are judgments about Babylon, Isaiah 13:1. Remember also that prophecy is not written in plain language, but in prophetic and symbolic language. Angels are used as message bearers; the sun, moon, and stars are sources or reflectors of light; and so on.

All through the thirteenth and fourteenth chapters we see either judgment on Judah through their conquest by Babylon or describing the deliverance of Judah from Babylonian bondage. In either case the subject is Babylon.

First, let's read the scriptural text.

Isaiah 13-14: "**The burden of Babylon**, which Isaiah the son of Amoz did see. Lift ye up a banner upon the high mountain, exalt the voice unto them, shake the hand, that they may go into the gates of the nobles. I have commanded my sanctified ones, I have also called my mighty ones for mine anger, even them that rejoice in my highness. The noise of a multitude in the mountains, like as of a great people; a tumultuous noise of the kingdoms of nations gathered together: the Lord of hosts mustered the host of the battle. They come from a far country, from the end of heaven, even the Lord, and the weapons of his indignation, to destroy the whole land.

Howl ye; for the day of the Lord is at hand; it shall come as a destruction from the Almighty. Therefore shall all hands be faint, and every man's heart shall melt: And they shall be afraid: pangs and sorrows shall take hold of them; they shall be in pain as a woman that travaileth: they shall be amazed one at another; their faces shall be as flames. Behold, the day of the Lord cometh, cruel both with wrath and fierce anger, to lay the land desolate: and he shall destroy the sinners thereof out of it. For the stars of heaven and the constellations thereof shall not give their light: the sun shall be darkened in his going forth, and the moon shall not cause her light to shine.

And I will punish the world for their evil, and the wicked for their iniquity; and I will cause the arrogancy of the proud to cease, and will lay low the haughtiness of the terrible. I will make a man more precious than fine gold; even a man than the golden wedge of Ophir. Therefore I will shake the heavens, and the earth shall remove out of her place, in the wrath of the Lord of hosts, and in the day of his fierce anger. And it shall be as the chased roe, and as a sheep that no man taketh up: they shall every man turn to his own people, and flee every one into his own land. Every one that is found shall be thrust through; and every one that is joined unto them shall fall by the sword. Their children also shall be dashed to pieces before their eyes; their houses shall be spoiled, and their wives ravished.

*B*ehold, I will stir up the Medes against them, which shall not regard silver; and as for gold, they shall not delight in it. Their bows also shall dash the young men to pieces; and they shall have no pity on the fruit of the womb; their eye shall not spare children. And Babylon, the glory of kingdoms, the beauty of the Chaldees' excellency, shall be as when God overthrew Sodom and Gomorrah. It shall never be inhabited, neither shall it be dwelt in from generation to generation: neither shall the Arabian pitch tent there; neither shall the shepherds make their fold there. But wild beasts of the desert shall lie there; and their houses shall be full of doleful creatures; and owls shall dwell there, and satyrs shall dance there. And the wild beasts of the islands shall cry in their desolate houses, and dragons in their pleasant palaces: and her time is near to come, and her days shall not be prolonged.

Isaiah 14: For the Lord will have mercy on Jacob, and will yet choose Israel, and set them in their own land: and the strangers shall be joined with them, and they shall cleave to the house of Jacob. And the people shall take them, and bring them to their place: and the house of Israel shall possess them in the land of the Lord for servants and handmaids: and they shall take them captives, whose captives they were; and they shall rule over their oppressors.

"And it shall come to pass in the day that the Lord shall give thee rest from thy sorrow, and from thy fear, and from the hard bondage wherein thou wast made to serve, *That thou shalt take up this proverb against the king of Babylon, and say, How hath the oppressor ceased! the golden city ceased!* The Lord hath broken the staff of the wicked, and the sceptre of the rulers. He who smote the people in wrath with a continual stroke, he that ruled the nations in anger, is persecuted, and none hindereth. The whole earth is at rest, and is quiet: they break forth into singing. Yea, the fir trees rejoice at thee, and the cedars of Lebanon, saying, Since thou art laid down, no feller is come up against us. Hell from beneath is moved for thee to meet thee at thy coming: it stirreth up the dead for thee, even all the chief ones of the earth; it hath raised up from their thrones all the kings of the nations.

All they shall speak and say unto thee, Art thou also become weak as we? art thou become like unto us? Thy pomp is brought down to the grave, and the noise of thy viols: the worm is spread under thee, and the worms cover thee. How art thou fallen from heaven, O Lucifer, son of the morning! how art thou cut down to the ground, which didst weaken the nations! For thou hast said in thine heart, I will ascend into heaven, I will exalt my throne above the stars of God: I will sit also upon the mount of the congregation, in the sides of the north: I will ascend above the heights of the clouds; I will be like the most High. Yet thou shalt be brought down to hell, to the sides of the pit. They that see thee shall narrowly look upon thee, and consider thee, saying, is this the man that made the earth to tremble, that did shake kingdoms; That made the world as a wilderness, and destroyed the cities thereof; that opened not the house of his prisoners?

All the kings of the nations, even all of them, lie in glory, every one in his own house. But thou art cast out of thy grave like an abominable branch, and as the raiment of those that are slain, thrust through with a sword, that go down to the stones of the pit; as a carcass trodden under feet. Thou shalt not be joined with them in burial, because thou hast destroyed thy land, and slain thy people: the seed of evildoers shall never be renowned. Prepare slaughter for his children for the iniquity of their fathers; that they do not rise, nor possess the land, nor fill the face of the world with cities.

For I will rise up against them, saith the Lord of hosts, and cut off from Babylon the name, and remnant, and son, and nephew, saith the Lord. I will also make it a possession for the bittern, and pools of water: and I will sweep it with the besom of destruction, saith the Lord of hosts. The Lord of hosts hath sworn, saying, Surely as I have thought, so shall it come to pass; and as I have purposed, so shall it stand: That I will break the Assyrian in my land, and upon my mountains tread him under foot: then shall his yoke depart from off them, and his burden depart from off their shoulders. This is the purpose that is purposed upon the whole earth: and this is the hand that is stretched out upon all the nations. For the Lord of hosts hath purposed, and who shall disannul it? and his hand is stretched out, and who shall turn it back?

In the year that king Ahaz died was this burden. Rejoice not thou, whole Palestina, because the rod of him that smote thee is broken: for out of the serpent's root shall come forth a cockatrice, and his fruit shall be a fiery flying serpent. And the firstborn of the poor shall feed, and the needy shall lie down in safety: and I will kill thy root with famine, and he shall slay thy remnant. Howl, O gate; cry, O city; thou, whole Palestina, art dissolved: for there shall come from the north a smoke, and none shall be alone in his appointed times. What shall one then answer the messengers of the nation? That the Lord hath founded Zion, and the poor of his people shall trust in it."

Now let's look at some key verses in the prophecy of Isaiah.

Isaiah 13:1: "**The burden of Babylon**, which Isaiah the son of Amoz did see."

This refers to the burden of, the problem of, or the message concerning Babylon. Although God had raised Babylon as a world power for the purpose of punishing Judah, Babylon was a tool in the hand of the Lord and not a child of His heart. After Babylon had fulfilled God's purpose, its residents were to be destroyed for their wickedness. Throughout Jewish history God used other nations as a tool of punishment for Israel's idolatry.

Isaiah 13:10: "For the stars of heaven and the constellations thereof shall not give their light: the sun shall be darkened in his going forth, and the moon shall not cause her light to shine."

In prophetic language, stars, sun, and moon are all light transmitters and angels are message bearers. The sun is the high originator of light, the stars are additional transmitters of light, and the moon is a reflector of the light given off by the sun. In the spiritual realm the sun would represent the light of God, Christ or the gospel. The entire Bible, Old and New Testaments, compose the Word or Light of God. The sun is the light of the gospel of Christ, the moon is the reflection of that light on the Old Testament, and the stars are angels, prophets, or ministers of the Word of God. All the focus of the Bible, Old and New Testaments, is the establishment of the kingdom of God through the Lord Jesus Christ. The apostle Paul also gave us to understand that the Old Testament was subordinate to the New, because the purpose of the Old is to bring us to the New.

Galatians 3:24-25 says, "Wherefore the law was our schoolmaster to bring us unto Christ, that we might be justified by faith. But after that faith is come, we are no longer under a schoolmaster."

This leads us to understand that the sun or (son) is the originator of light, and that light is the Lord Jesus Christ.

> "Then spake Jesus again unto them, saying, I am the light of
> the world: he that followeth me shall not walk in darkness,
> but shall have the light of life" (John 8:12).

Since Jesus, the new covenant, is the true source of light, the old covenant is the reflector of that light. As the sun is the originator and the major light, the moon is the lesser or the primary reflector of that light, identifying the Old Testament as necessary to the overall light of the gospel. The stars or transmitters of the light are the messengers of the gospel, the angels, the prophets, the apostles, and the modern ministry. As Abraham looked for a city that had foundations, he was looking forward to the building Jesus would establish, which is built on the foundation of the apostles and prophets.

The apostle Paul further reveals the structure of the church as a building with foundations. First of all, Abraham, the patriarch of promise, did not receive the fulfillment of promise in his lifetime. Paul says in Hebrews that he looked for a city:

> "By faith Abraham, when he was called to go out into a place which he should after receive for an inheritance, obeyed; and he went out, not knowing whither he went. By faith he sojourned in the land of promise, as in a strange country, dwelling in tabernacles with Isaac and Jacob, the heirs with him of the same promise: For he looked for a *city which hath foundations*, whose builder and maker is God" (Hebrews 11:8-10).

Paul then identifies the city as the kingdom of God, or the church that Jesus said that He would build and said the gates of hell would not prevail against it.

> "Now therefore ye are no more strangers and foreigners, but fellow citizens with the saints, and of the household of God; And are built upon the foundation of the apostles and prophets, Jesus Christ himself being the chief corner stone" (Ephesians 2:19-20).

So, the church that Jesus built is built upon the foundation of the apostles and prophets with Jesus Christ as the cornerstone. The moon is the greatest reflector of God's light, which is the old covenant or the Law of Moses and the prophets.

Now let's look at the metaphor of the church in Revelation 12: "And there appeared a great wonder in heaven; a woman clothed with the sun, and the moon under her feet, and upon her head a crown of twelve stars: And she being with child cried, travailing in birth, and pained to be delivered" (Revelation 12:1-2).

Heaven in this context is not the heaven of eternal bliss. It is the kingdom of God or the church. Here we have the infant church or the apostolic church travailing to bring forth new life through the gospel of Christ. This church is the Bride of Christ and in the apostolic time she was very pregnant, agonizing to give birth. She, the Church, is seen as being "clothed with the sun," that is, bathed in the glory of God and the gospel, the first and primary element in the foundation of the Church. She was standing on the moon. The Old Testament or the Law and the prophets were the schoolmaster to bring us to Christ. So the moon is the second element in that foundation. Jesus Christ, "the Word," the anchoring stone that binds together all the Word of God spoken by the prophets and the words spoken by the Lord through the apostles, creating that building that we know as "the building of God," is the third element in the foundation.

Ephesians 2:20 says, "And are built upon the foundation of the apostles and prophets, Jesus Christ himself being the chief corner stone."

These two foundation elements are tied together by the cornerstone Jesus Christ. We went through this exercise to show that sun, moon, stars, and angels are metaphors and not meant literally. If we keep this in mind and focus on the context of the scripture, all this becomes apparent.

> "Behold, I will stir up the Medes against them, which shall not regard silver; and as for gold, they shall not delight in it. Their bows also shall dash the young men to pieces; and

they shall have no pity on the fruit of the womb; their eye shall not spare children. *And Babylon, the glory of kingdoms, the beauty of the Chaldees' excellency, shall be as when God overthrew Sodom and Gomorrah.* It shall never be inhabited, neither shall it be dwelt in from generation to generation: neither shall the Arabian pitch tent there; neither shall the shepherds make their fold there" (Isaiah 13:17-20).

Here we see Babylonian history unfold. It was God who raised up this kingdom for a purpose, and now God is going to bring it down since His purpose has been fulfilled. God said he would "stir up the Medes" against them. Remember, the third king of Babylon, Belshazzar, held a feast and polluted the vessels of the Lord's temple by drinking wine from them. Then came the handwriting on the wall and judgment was pronounced on Babylon. (See Daniel 5.) Darius the Mede entered Babylon that very night, slew the king, and ruled. Babylon as a world power was gone forever in one night.

Now let's identify specifically who Lucifer is by examining two places in Isaiah:

"That thou shalt take up this proverb against the king of Babylon, and say, How hath the oppressor ceased! the golden city ceased!" (Isaiah 14:4).

"Thy pomp is brought down to the grave, and the noise of thy viols: the worm is spread under thee, and the worms cover thee. How art thou fallen from heaven, O Lucifer, son of the morning! how art thou cut down to the ground, which didst weaken the nations! For thou hast said in thine heart, I will ascend into heaven, I will exalt my throne above the stars of God: I will sit also upon the mount of the congregation, in the sides of the north: I will ascend above the heights of the clouds; I will be like the most High. Yet thou shalt be brought down to hell, to the sides of the pit. They that see thee shall narrowly look upon thee, and

consider thee, saying, Is this the man that made the earth
to tremble, that did shake kingdoms" (Isaiah 14:11-16).

In verse 4 Isaiah is instructed to "take up this proverb against the *king
of Babylon.*" We are not talking about Babylon only but specifically
the king of Babylon. The demise of this kingdom is expressed as a
question. How hath the oppressor ceased! the golden city ceased! The
oppressor is Nebuchadnezzar, and the golden city is Babylon.

In verse 11, "thy pomp is brought down to the grave." Nebuchadnezzar
ruled and provided for many peoples. (Notice Nebuchadnezzar's
dream in Daniel 4 included below.) We see that Nebuchadnezzar was
appointed by God to rise up in power to conquer Judah as punishment
for her idolatry. Like many powerful leaders, Nebuchadnezzar
attributed his rise to power to his own glory, and God brought Babylon
and its king to judgment. In Nebuchadnezzar's dreams he saw a great
tree that was a representation of the king himself. Then in his dream
he saw an ax man who was commanded to hew down the tree yet
leave the stump so that after a time the kingdom would be restored to
Nebuchadnezzar. Nebuchadnezzar was brought to judgment because
his pride and arrogance propelled him to take credit for his prosperity
rather than give honor and glory to God, who raised him up as a world
power. God took his reason from him and he grazed in the field like an
animal until he came to realize the authority of God in the kingdoms
of men. When his reason returned, he honored the sovereign God of
heaven as the one God who gives and takes the kingdoms of men at
His own will.

Now let's reason in the scriptures.

> Verse 13 says, "I will ascend into heaven," Lucifer's own
> words declare "I will ascend." How can one ascend when
> he is already there and being cast down? By these words
> alone Lucifer tells us he was not in heaven.

Verse 28 says "In the year that king Ahaz died was this burden". Think about it. If the account of Lucifer was recorded in the year king Ahaz died, Satan could not have existed before that time and therefore could not have been in the garden to tempt Eve. Remember, prophecy does not report the past but the future.

Verse 12 says, "How art thou fallen from heaven O Lucifer?" Prophetically heaven or mountains typically refer to nations, kingdoms, and high authority. Jesus spoke consistently about the kingdom of heaven interchangeably with the kingdom of God. This heaven was not the heavenly abode of the Father but the spiritual reigning of God's people. Notice also that this Lucifer is said to have weakened the nations. If this Lucifer had been in the garden as the serpent how could he have weakened the nations as no nations existed at that time. Again, if Lucifer was an angel cast down from heaven, his casting out had to have occurred before meeting Eve in the garden.

Nebuchadnezzar had been elevated by God to be the ruler of the nations of the east. Since Nebuchadnezzar was ruling under God's anointing his kingdom and ruler ship is prophetically heaven. When Lucifer or rather Nebuchadnezzar was cast out of heaven, it was the losing of his God appointed authority to rule over the people of God. We further see Nebuchadnezzar as the Lucifer of this text in verse 16, where the question is asked, Is this the man that made the earth to tremble? Therefore, Lucifer is not an angel but a man and that man is Nebuchadnezzar the king of Babylon.

The entire fourth chapter of Daniel is included below. It is Nebuchadnezzar's personal testimony concerning his God-given authority over God's nations, his insanity, and his restoration and acknowledgment of God's power over the nations.

Daniel 4

"Nebuchadnezzar the king, unto all people, nations, and languages, that dwell in all the earth; Peace be multiplied unto you. I thought it good to shew the signs and wonders that the high God hath wrought toward me. How great are his signs! and how mighty are his wonders! his kingdom is an everlasting kingdom, and his dominion is from generation to generation. I Nebuchadnezzar was at rest in mine house, and flourishing in my palace: I saw a dream which made me afraid, and the thoughts upon my bed and the visions of my head troubled me.

Therefore made I a decree to bring in all the wise men of Babylon before me, that they might make known unto me the interpretation of the dream. Then came in the magicians, the astrologers, the Chaldeans, and the soothsayers: and I told the dream before them; but they did not make known unto me the interpretation thereof. But at the last Daniel came in before me, whose name was Belteshazzar, according to the name of my god, and in whom is the spirit of the holy gods: and before him I told the dream, saying, O Belteshazzar, master of the magicians, because I know that the spirit of the holy gods is in thee, and no secret troubleth thee, tell me the visions of my dream that I have seen, and the interpretation thereof.

Thus were the visions of mine head in my bed; I saw, and behold a tree in the midst of the earth, and the height thereof was great. The tree grew, and was strong, and the height thereof reached unto heaven, and the sight thereof to the end of all the earth: The leaves thereof were fair, and the fruit thereof much, and in it was meat for all: the beasts of the field had shadow under it, and the fowls of the heaven dwelt in the boughs thereof, and all flesh was fed of it. I saw in the visions of my head upon my bed, and, behold, a watcher and an holy one came down from heaven; He cried aloud, and said thus, Hew down the tree, and cut off his branches, shake off his leaves, and scatter his fruit: let the beasts get away from under it, and the fowls from his branches: Nevertheless leave the stump of his roots in the earth, even with a band of iron and brass, in the tender grass of the field; and let it be wet with the dew of heaven, and let his portion be with the beasts in the grass of the earth:

Let his heart be changed from man's, and let a beast's heart be given unto him; and let seven times pass over him. This matter is by the decree of the watchers, and the demand by the word of the holy ones: to the intent that the living may know that the most High ruleth in the kingdom of men, and giveth it to whomsoever he will, and setteth up over it the basest of men. This dream I king Nebuchadnezzar have seen. Now thou, O Belteshazzar, declare the interpretation thereof, forasmuch as all the wise men of my kingdom are not able to make known unto me the interpretation: but thou art able; for the spirit of the holy gods is in thee. Then Daniel, whose name was Belteshazzar, was astonied for one hour, and his thoughts troubled him. The king spake, and said, Belteshazzar, let not the dream, or the interpretation thereof, trouble thee. Belteshazzar answered and said, My lord, the dream be to them that hate thee, and the interpretation thereof to thine enemies.

The tree that thou sawest, which grew, and was strong, whose height reached unto the heaven, and the sight thereof to all the earth; Whose leaves were fair, and the fruit thereof much, and in it was meat for all; under which the beasts of the field dwelt, and upon whose branches the fowls of the heaven had their habitation: It is thou, O king, that art grown and become strong: for thy greatness is grown, and reacheth unto heaven, and thy dominion to the end of the earth. And whereas the king saw a watcher and an holy one coming down from heaven, and saying, Hew the tree down, and destroy it; yet leave the stump of the roots thereof in the earth, even with a band of iron and brass, in the tender grass of the field; and let it be wet with the dew of heaven, and let his portion be with the beasts of the field, till seven times pass over him; This is the interpretation, O king, and this is the decree of the most High, which is come upon my lord the king: That they shall drive thee from men, and thy dwelling shall be with the beasts of the field, and they shall make thee to eat grass as oxen, and they shall wet thee with the dew of heaven, and seven times shall pass over thee, till thou know that the most High ruleth in the kingdom of men, and giveth it to whomsoever he will.

And whereas they commanded to leave the stump of the tree roots; thy kingdom shall be sure unto thee, after that thou shalt have known that the heavens do rule. Wherefore, O king, let my counsel be acceptable unto thee, and break off thy sins by righteousness, and thine iniquities by shewing mercy to the poor; if it may be a lengthening of thy tranquillity. All this came upon the king Nebuchadnezzar. At the end of twelve months he walked in the palace of the kingdom of Babylon. The king spake, and said, Is not this great Babylon, that I have built for the house of the kingdom by the might of my power, and for the honour of my majesty?

While the word was in the king's mouth, there fell a voice from heaven, saying, *O king Nebuchadnezzar, to thee it is spoken; The kingdom is departed from thee. And they shall drive thee from men, and thy dwelling shall be with the beasts of the field: they shall make thee to eat grass as oxen, and seven times shall pass over thee, until thou know that the most High ruleth in the kingdom of men, and giveth it to whomsoever he will.* The same hour was the thing fulfilled upon Nebuchadnezzar: and he was driven from men, and did eat grass as oxen, and his body was wet with the dew of heaven, till his hairs were grown like eagles' feathers, and his nails like birds' claws. *And at the end of the days I Nebuchadnezzar lifted up mine eyes unto heaven, and mine understanding returned unto me, and I blessed the most High, and I praised and honoured him that liveth for ever, whose dominion is an everlasting dominion, and his kingdom is from generation to generation:*

And all the inhabitants of the earth are reputed as nothing: and he doeth according to his will in the army of heaven, and among the inhabitants of the earth: and none can stay his hand, or say unto him, What doest thou? At the same time my reason returned unto me; and for the glory of my kingdom, mine honour and brightness returned unto me; and my counsellors and my lords sought unto me; and I was established in my kingdom, and excellent majesty was added unto me. Now I Nebuchadnezzar praise and extol and honour the King of heaven, all whose works are truth, and his ways judgment: and those that walk in pride he is able to abase."

The above scripture is Nebuchadnezzar's personal account of having received of God a kingdom, power, and rule over God's people. When he tried to take credit for his prosperity, God pulled his reasoning from his mind and he went insane. After a period his reasoning returned, and he confessed that God truly ruled in the kingdoms of men. It is this period of insanity that is referred to in the question "How art thou fallen from heaven O Lucifer." Attempting to make Satan a fallen angel violates all spiritual reason. Is God omnipotent or not? Is God sovereign or not?

There is also an attempt to apply Luke 17:20 to the concept of Lucifer falling from heaven. Jesus spoke these words on the return of the disciples from a preaching mission.

"And the seventy returned again with joy, saying, Lord, even the devils are subject unto us through thy name. And he said unto them, I beheld Satan as lightning fall from heaven. Behold, I give unto you power to tread on serpents and scorpions, and over all the power of the enemy: and nothing shall by any means hurt you. Notwithstanding in this rejoice not, that the spirits are subject unto you; but rather rejoice, because your names are written in heaven" (Luke 10:17-20).

The following is an article taken from the Pulpit commentary

Luke 10:17; Luke 10:18; Luke 10:19

Verse 17: "And the seventy returned again with joy, saying, Lord, even the devils are subject unto us through thy Name."

How wavering and hesitating the faith of the chosen followers of Jesus was. Even at this late period of his public ministry, it is clear from this frank confession of surprise at their powers. They were contrasting the present with what had lately happened at the foot of the Mount of Transfiguration, where the disciples were utterly unable to heal the possessed boy. What a contrast these true writers of the gospel story paint between themselves and their master! They never seem to tire in their self-depreciatory descriptions. They describe with the same careful, truthful pen their slowness to understand what afterward became so clear to them: their mutual jealousies, their covetous hopes of a brilliant future, their shrinking from pain and suffering, their utter failure when they tried to imitate their master. Now we find them marveling at their own—to them—unexpected success in their imitation of him.

Verse 18: "And he said unto them, I beheld Satan as lightning fall from heaven." The Lord's words here were prophetic rather than descriptive of what had taken or was then taking place. The seventy were telling him their feelings of joy at finding that his name in their mouths enabled them to cast out evil spirits from the possessed. Their master replied in an exalted and exultant strain—strange and rare sounds on the lips of the man of sorrows—telling them how he had been looking—not on a few spirits of evil driven out of unhappy men, but on the king and chief of all evil falling from his sad eminence and throne of power like a flash of lightning. Jesus Christ saw, in the first success of these poor servants of his, an earnest of that wonderful and mighty victory that his followers, simply armed with the power of his name, would shortly win over paganism. He saw, too, in the dim far future, many a contest with and victory over evil in its many forms. He looked on, we may well believe, to the final defeat, which at length his servants, when they should have learned the true use and the resistless power of that glorious name of his, should win over the restless enemy of the souls of men.

Verse 19: Behold, I give unto you power to tread on serpents and scorpions, and over all the power of the enemy. The older authorities read here, "I have given." The only recorded instance of a literal fulfillment of this promise was in the case of Paul at Melina, after the shipwreck (Acts 24:3-5). A similar promise was made during the "forty days" (Mark 16:17-18). It seems however, best, in the case of this peculiar promise, to interpret the Lord's words as referring to spiritual powers of evil, taking the serpent and scorpion as symbols of these. It should be remembered that the subject of conversation between the master and his servants was the conflict with and victory ever these awful powers restlessly hostile to the human race (see Psalm 91:13).

(From The Pulpit Commentary, Electronic Database, 2010 © 2001, 2003, 2005, 2006, 2010 by Biblesoft, Inc. All rights reserved.)

This commentary is very clear on the subject. Jesus was not watching Satan being cast out of the heaven of God's abode, but out of ruling authority over the people of God. Until Jesus infused the spiritual authority in the hearts of the disciples, Satan basically ruled in the kingdoms of men. The writer of the commentary says that the power that the disciples experienced over sickness and evil spirits was only the "earnest" or "down payment" of the power that the people of God would possess "after that the Holy Ghost came upon them." Satan is described by the apostle Paul as "*the god of this world.*"

Second Corinthians 4:4 says, "In whom the god of this world hath blinded the minds of them which believe not, lest the light of the glorious gospel of Christ, who is the image of God, should shine unto them."

With the inauguration of the church that Jesus built, the infilling of the Holy Spirit into the hearts of the people of God, and the discovery by the disciples that the name of Jesus instilled them with power over all Satan's devices, Satan's power to rule in the lives of men was broken and truly he fell from his place of power in this world and became subject to the authority of the people of God through faith in the name of the Lord Jesus Christ.

CHAPTER FIFTEEN

Millennium

Another greatly misunderstood Bible doctrine is that of the millennium. Several words can be used in place of the actual word millennium. Some of those words are time, age, eon, eternity, and a thousand years. The word millennium does not appear in the Bible. Bible expositors, when using the term millennium, are making reference to "one thousand years" found in Revelation 20:1-7

> And I saw an angel come down from heaven, having the key of the bottomless pit and a great chain in his hand. And he laid hold on the dragon, that old serpent, which is the Devil, and Satan, and bound him a thousand years, And cast him into the bottomless pit, and shut him up, and set a seal upon him, that he should deceive the nations no more, till the thousand years should be fulfilled: and after that he must be loosed a little season. And I saw thrones, and they sat upon them, and judgment was given unto them: and I saw the souls of them that were beheaded for the witness of Jesus, and for the word of God, and which had not worshipped the beast, neither his image, neither had received his mark upon their foreheads, or in their hands; and they lived and reigned with Christ a thousand years. But the rest of the dead lived not again until the thousand years were finished. This is the first resurrection. Blessed and holy is he that hath part in the first resurrection: on such

the second death hath no power, but they shall be priests
of God and of Christ, and shall reign with him a thousand
years. And when the thousand years are expired, Satan shall
be loosed out of his prison. (Revelation 20:1-7)

In the preceding scripture verses, we have the fundamental scripture
used to teach the doctrine of the millennium, or the thousand-years
reign of Christ on the earth. The popular version of the doctrine says
that Christ will return and "rapture" His people from off the earth. The
people remaining on earth will then have a brief time of tribulation
followed by a general return of Christ "with" His followers to set up an
earthly kingdom in Jerusalem and there reign with His saints for one
thousand years, after which Satan will be freed from the bottomless pit
to again inflict malice on the inhabitants of the earth.

There are several problems with the preceding application of the
scriptures contained in chapter 20 of Revelation. One very glaring
problem is the return of Christ. Nowhere in the Bible is there any
hint that Christ will return more than once. I heard one minister who
was teaching on the millennium say that in order for the doctrine of
pre-millennialism to work, there would have to be several returns of
Christ to be able to accomplish the different phases of the millennial
doctrine. The minister who was teaching this lesson was in favor of the
doctrine of the millennium but confessed he was unable to determine
exactly how many times Jesus would have to return to complete Bible
prophecy. Doesn't that make an uncertain sound? If we cannot clearly
determine how many times Christ will return, how will we be able to
be properly prepared, and how can we alert others of the promises and
the dangers?

The following scriptures all describe the "last day." I realize that in
eternity, there is no passing of time. Trying to imagine the length of
eternity in years is an exercise in futility since there will not be any
years. Christ is the light illuminating heaven, and as such, that light
never goes out, leaving eternity as a never-ending day. However, we
do now live in a time-controlled element. This world had a beginning

and will end. Our lives had a beginning and will end. There is only one starting and one ending. I was born and I will die. When I take my last breath, that will be the "last" day of my life, and I will do it only once. There cannot be anything after the "last" day. The "last" day is the end and what can come after it? Jesus declared He would raise His followers on the "last" day. Jesus said nothing about a rapture or preliminary resurrection for the just a thousand years before the resurrection of the unjust. Once a man dies, his next stop is the judgment.

Hebrews 9:27 says, "And as it is appointed unto men once to die, but after this the judgment."

Now read these scripture texts:

> "And this is the Father's will which hath sent me, that of all which he hath given me I should lose nothing, but should raise it up again at the last day" (John 6:39).

> "And this is the will of him that sent me, that every one which seeth the Son, and believeth on him, may have everlasting life: and I will raise him up at the last day" (John 6:40).

> "No man can come to me, except the Father which hath sent me draw him: and I will raise him up at the last day" (John 6:44).

> "Whoso eateth my flesh, and drinketh my blood, hath eternal life; and I will raise him up at the last day" (John 6:54).

> "Martha saith unto him, I know that he shall rise again in the resurrection at the last day" (John 11:24).

> "He that rejecteth me, and receiveth not my words, hath one that judgeth him: the word that I have spoken, the same shall judge him in the last day" (John 12:48).

As can be clearly seen, the resurrection and the last day occur at the same time. But the question might be asked, Won't the just be resurrected before the unjust? No. Read the next set of scriptures.

"Marvel not at this: for the hour is coming, in the which all that are in the graves shall hear his voice, And shall come forth; they that have done good, unto the resurrection of life; and they that have done evil, unto the resurrection of damnation" (John 5:28-29).

"And have hope toward God, which they themselves also allow, that there shall be a resurrection of the dead, both of the just and unjust" (Acts 24:15).

The foregoing verses clearly declare that there will be a general resurrection of the just and the unjust alike. One of the scriptures used to prove the rapture is 1 Thessalonians 4:17. The doctrine of the rapture will be dealt with in the chapter on that subject.

First Thessalonians 4:14-17 says, "For if we believe that Jesus died and rose again, even so them also which sleep in Jesus will God bring with him. [Those who are asleep in Jesus are those who 'died saved]. For this we say unto you by the word of the Lord, that we which are alive and remain unto the coming of the Lord shall not prevent them which are asleep. [Those who are alive and remain are those still living at the last day. Christians still alive when Christ returns will not interfere with the coming of those departed and in their graves]. For the Lord himself shall descend from heaven with a shout, with the voice of the archangel, and with the trump of God: and the dead in Christ shall rise first: [At the resurrection of the last day, the dead in Christ will come forth from the graves.] Then we which are alive and remain shall be caught up together with them in the clouds, to meet the Lord in the air: and so shall we ever be with the Lord."

Once the graves have delivered up their dead, the living will join them and together they will be transported to heaven, "caught up together into the clouds to meet the Lord in the air," and then the scripture says "so shall we ever be with the Lord." These verses do not declare that anyone neither man, angel, Christ nor anyone else will ever return to Jerusalem to set up a kingdom and rule in the earth. Rather, it says we will all be caught up into the air and so "ever be with the Lord." The scriptures declare that we will meet Jesus in the air, or heaven, not on the ground or earth and "so shall we ever be with the Lord." The truth of the matter is that the kingdom of God is not and will never be in Jerusalem. Listen to Jesus: "Neither shall they say, Lo here! or, lo there! for, behold, the kingdom of God is within you" (Luke 17:21).

The Bottomless Pit

There are seven verses of scripture in the Bible referring to the bottomless pit. You will notice that the scriptures in Revelation 20 are related to the binding of Satan and sealing him in the bottomless pit, and the others are in chapters 9, 11, and 17 and relate to the loosing of Satan from the bottomless pit. Those who take the interpretation of the Revelation literally seem to have gotten the cart before the horse. Why would we "loose" Satan before we "bind" him? The Revelation is not a literal book, but a spiritual and symbolic book. It is not a book for the general world, but one for the people of God. It is a revealing of the spiritual nature and condition of the church to the church.

Revelation 1:1 says, "*The Revelation of Jesus Christ,* which God gave unto him, *to shew unto his servants* things which must shortly come to pass; and he sent and signified it by his angel unto his servant John."

The apostle Paul admonished Timothy to study in order to "rightly" divide the word of truth. "Study to shew thyself approved unto God, a workman that needeth not to be ashamed, rightly dividing the word of truth" (2 Timothy 2:15).

There is a right and a wrong way to assemble the word of truth. Revelation is not a novel beginning at chapter 1 and ending with chapter 22. Instead, Revelation is a series of messages to be delivered to the seven churches of Revelation. The entire book is divided into seven series of events, each spanning the entire gospel day. Since Christ has only one church, the seven churches of Revelation must represent some portion of that one church. When we rightly divide the Revelation, we divide the gospel day into seven periods of time and place one of the seven churches into each one, making one and the same church passing through the seven spiritual phases of the gospel day. The seven angels are the messengers or ministry of the seven churches. These angels are not literally seven, but the ministry with its particular message to the church during its administration. Again, the seven trumpets is the message proclaimed by this angel in its respective period of time. Thus, the first angel blows the first trumpet in the first period of time and so forth. When we divide Revelation in this way and then compare it with recorded history, we have perfect harmony between the Bible and the historical events in their respective periods of time throughout the gospel day.

The binding of Satan in Revelation 20 does not refer to binding him with a literal chain and throwing him in a literal hole, but rather binding his ability to deceive the nations.

> "And I saw an angel come down from heaven, having the key of the bottomless pit and a great chain in his hand. . . . And cast him into the bottomless pit, and shut him up, and set a seal upon him, that he should deceive the nations no more, till the thousand years should be fulfilled: and after that he must be loosed a little season" (Revelation 20:1, 3).

The Smyrna church, the second of the seven churches of Asia, was told they should look forward to ten days of tribulation in this passage: "Fear none of those things which thou shalt suffer: behold, the devil shall cast some of you into prison, that ye may be tried; and ye shall have tribulation ten days: be thou faithful unto death, and I will give thee a crown of life" (Revelation 2:10).

The Smyrna church follows the apostolic or first period of the gospel day, which is recognized as the time dating between 270 AD and 530 AD. Revelation is a book of symbols, and here we have the prophecy of ten days of tribulation. Using symbolic language, we apply each day as 100 years (10 x 100 = 1,000). This is precisely the time of the Dark Ages of Catholicism as a state religion, 530 AD to 1530 AD. Remember the Smyrna church was told that "ye shall have tribulation ten days" suggesting that those "ten days" would come in the following church period or the Pergamos period.

This period was truly a time of tribulation, as the Catholic Church waged war on every believer not surrendering to the deceptions of Rome. Persecution, torture and murder were the order of the day. (Note: Read Fox's book of martyrs. Written by John Foxe during the sixteenth century) The crime that these saints were charged with was not being a Catholic. Historically, this thousand years agrees with Bible prophecy as 530 AD-1530 AD, a millennium.

During the period of the Dark Ages, AD 530-AD 1530, Catholicism ruled supreme. Although there were a few genuine Christians in that time, they were a "remnant" holding on to saving grace. The Catholic Church had thrown away spiritual transformation in exchange for rites and ritual, declaring that sins were pardonable by the priesthood. Christ was effectively removed from the saving transaction, and thereby salvation was removed. The binding of Satan was that he would "deceive the nations *no more.*" The religious world was already deceived, but during that time of one thousand years of the Dark Ages, no other religious movements were formed. Satan was truly bound from sending forth any "other forms of deception" during the one thousand years of Catholic dominion. The chain and the keys are the Word of God.

Matthew 16:19 says, "And I will give unto thee the keys of the kingdom of heaven: and whatsoever thou shalt bind on earth shall be bound in heaven: and whatsoever thou shalt loose on earth shall be loosed in heaven."

And Revelation 1:18 says, "I am he that liveth, and was dead; and, behold, I am alive for evermore, Amen; and have the keys of hell and of death."

Neither can Satan be kept in a bottomless pit since there is no such thing as a bottomless pit on this earth. Remember, if you dig far enough, you will again reach the surface. The concept of "bottomless" simply exposes that the doctrines that come from the world (men) have no foundation or basis in truth. Any doctrine founded on any other source than the Word of God is without foundation or false and has no supporting basis and therefore is a lie. The apostle Paul makes this point very clear in the following passages:

> "According to the grace of God which is given unto me, as a wise masterbuilder, I have laid the foundation, and another buildeth thereon. But let every man take heed how he buildeth thereupon. For other foundation can no man lay than that is laid, which is Jesus Christ" (1 Corinthians 3:10-11).

> "And they had a king over them, which is the angel of the bottomless pit, whose name in the Hebrew tongue is Abaddon, but in the Greek tongue hath his name Apollyon" (Revelation 9:11).

The angel of the bottomless pit is Satan, and his angels are the false prophets or the ministry of man-ruled religious movements. This false ministry is the "fallen angels" mentioned above.

During the one thousand years of the Dark Ages the people of God held on to their salvation by the mercy and grace of God through faith in the saving blood of the Lord Jesus Christ and the leadership of the Holy Spirit. Even though Satan ruled in the religious systems of men, those genuinely saved were truly living and reigning with Christ during this period of papal darkness, primarily because they were not bombarded by new deceptions. Christ had bound Satan in the bottomless pit of Catholicism. Those who had not bowed to the pope truly lived and reigned with Christ for this one thousand years. They experienced genuine heart-changing salvation.

Revelation 11:7 says, "And when they shall have finished their testimony, the beast that ascendeth out of the bottomless pit shall make war against them, and shall overcome them, and kill them."

The reference to *they* in the preceding verse refers to the two witnesses mentioned in Revelation 11:3, the "Word" and the "Spirit." The beast is the devouring religious systems that come from the earth (men), not from heaven (Word of God). When man takes it upon himself to alter, adjust, add to, or delete from the Word of God, the Holy Spirit is refused as the interpreter of the scriptures and men replace the doctrines of God with their own ideas, concepts, and beliefs. Thus, the Word of God and the influence of the Holy Spirit become ineffective and are killed to them.

During the one thousand years of Catholic rule, the Word of God and the Holy Spirit (the two witnesses) were actively alive in the souls of the remnant of God's people. And they lived and reigned with Christ during these one thousand years (530 AD-1530 AD). After this one thousand years Satan is loosed, and with a vengeance he floods the world with sectarian division and a multiplicity of deceptive denominations.

Consider the following passages:

> "Howbeit when he, the Spirit of truth, is come, he will guide you into all truth: for he shall not speak of himself; but whatsoever he shall hear, that shall he speak: and he will shew you things to come" (John 16:13).

> "We are of God: he that knoweth God heareth us; he that is not of God heareth not us. Hereby know we the spirit of truth, and the spirit of error" (1 John 4:6).

Another glaring problem is holding Satan with a literal chain. Satan is a spirit and cannot be contained by natural fetters. There is no question that Jesus had and continues to have absolute power over Satan. Whenever Jesus commanded the evil spirit to depart from a person, the evil spirit departed. When Jesus confronted Satan in the wilderness, He defeated him by use of the scriptures. Jesus also gave His disciples power over Satan to cast him out of those so afflicted. Satan was and is bound by the Word of God. The keys to the bottomless pit are also the aforementioned keys of heaven and hell, which are the Word of God and the gospel of the Lord Jesus Christ. When God binds Satan's power, he is bound indeed. As related above, God bound Satan's ability to deceive in any additional manner during the one thousand years. Deceptions already in place remained, but no new deceptions were adopted during the one thousand years. Satan was truly bound. Placing a seal on Satan is the authority of God in this binding of Satan. No man, religion, or any other power will be able to remove the binding power of God. By the power of the Word of God, Satan is bound for the one thousand years, and after that, he is loosed for a little season. During the one thousand years, the period of Catholic power (530 AD-1530 AD), Satan was bound up within the bottomless pit of Catholicism. At the conclusion of that period, the sixteenth-century Reformation, Satan was loosed, and from that time till now the array of confusing denominations and religions is overwhelming. Once Satan was able to corrupt religious minds, he came on with a vengeance, because he knows his opportunity is limited, as it says in Revelation 12:12: "Therefore rejoice, ye heavens, and ye that dwell in them. Woe to the inhabiters of the earth and of the sea! for the devil is come down unto you, having great wrath, because he knoweth that he hath but a short time."

Lastly on this subject are the first and second resurrection and the first and second death, which are taught in the scriptures. Notice the following passages:

> "He that hath an ear, let him hear what the Spirit saith
> unto the churches; He that overcometh shall not be hurt of
> the second death" (Revelation 2:11).

The preceding verse is written to the church, so the Revelation message is going out to Christian people. There is no mention of any resurrection but only of the second death. The first resurrection has already occurred: the raising of the soul from death to life through the saving grace of Jesus Christ.

> "We know that we have passed from death unto life, because we love the brethren" (1 John 3:14).

The earthly state of man is a condition of spiritual death. Listen to the apostle Paul in his own experience. When Jesus comes into the heart, this soul of ours, which is dead in trespasses and sins, is resurrected in newness of life. "For I was alive without the law once: but when the commandment came, sin revived, and I died. And the commandment, which was ordained to life, I found to be unto death. For sin, taking occasion by the commandment, deceived me, and by it slew me" (Romans 7:9-11).

> "Blessed and holy is he that hath part in the first resurrection: on such the second death hath no power, but they shall be priests of God and of Christ, and shall reign with him a thousand years" (Revelation 20:6).

> "And death and hell were cast into the lake of fire. This is the second death" (Revelation 20:14).

> "But the fearful, and unbelieving, and the abominable, and murderers, and whoremongers, and sorcerers, and idolaters, and all liars, shall have their part in the lake which burneth with fire and brimstone: which is the second death" (Revelation 21:8).

In the preceding verses, the second death is the lake of fire or final judgment. At the general resurrection at the last day all that are in the graves, bad and good, will come forth. This is the second resurrection for those who are saved by the blood of Jesus Christ and the first resurrection for the unjust. The first resurrection for the saved was at their conversion into saving grace. Those who have partaken of the saving grace of Christ will not be affected by the second death, which is the final judgment of the lake of fire reserved for the devil and his angels. The ungodly are dead already in trespasses and sins and will be resurrected at the general resurrection and ultimately cast into the lake of fire, the second death.

In brief:

1. The godly
   A. Their first resurrection is the transforming grace of God in saving the soul.
   B. Their second resurrection is at the general resurrection at the last day to eternal life.
   C. Their first death is the death of the body.
   D. They will not participate in the second death, which is only for the ungodly.

2. The ungodly
   A. These never participate in the resurrection of saving grace, but their first resurrection is the general resurrection at the last day.
   B. Their first death is the death of the body.
   C. Their second death is the lake of fire and eternal damnation.

CHAPTER SIXTEEN

Promiscuity

Indiscriminate, Immoral, Lewd, Careless, Licentious behavior

Promiscuity can be applied to many thoughts or subjects. Promiscuity describes careless and confused behavior, especially in sexual relations. Indiscriminate sexual activity exacts a terrible penalty. Modern society, to gain acceptance of our "sexual revolution," has used our own Constitution by misapplying several of its amendments, in particular, the First and Fourteenth, to include lewdness as "free speech," opening the doors for nudity, homosexuality, and pornography. Sixty years ago, these subjects were only whispered about in the back rooms of bars and other places of indecency. Today, many patrons of the bars are served by women who are bare breasted and in some cases, totally nude. The adult entertainment center has become a common site along our boulevards where women strip in front of the clientele, undulating in such a provocative manner that some of the men who view such behavior go out and find some outlet for their excitement. Sometimes that outlet ends up in some innocent woman's rape or a child's molestation and worse.

Because of the indiscriminate sexual activity during the past sixty years, a great majority of our society is infected with various venereal diseases. Syphilis and gonorrhea have been with us for centuries. Now we have AIDS, which is far worse than any of the earlier sexually transmitted diseases. AIDS is not only serious but can be fatal. Some progress is being made in the treatment of AIDS, but little hope of survival is offered to the afflicted. Since AIDS is a product of rampant homosexual activity, and homosexuality is protected by the First and Fourteenth Amendments, it becomes a violation of a person's constitutional rights to impose testing for the disease. For many years people applying for a marriage license have been required to be tested for venereal diseases that are treatable, but it is against their rights to have to be tested for AIDS. AIDS is treatable but not curable and when infected, many are doomed to a deteriorating life and premature death. Herpes is so common that it is estimated that a large percentage of our population is infected with this disease. Although it is treatable, it is not curable, and anyone with the disease can transmit it to his or her partners. What a price to pay for a little "liberty."

A great tragedy today is the effect this promiscuity has had on our younger generation. Sixty years ago, in most neighborhoods, our children could play outside after dark. Teenage girls many times babysat in their neighborhood and walked home after midnight without fear. Lost children could walk up to any adult and find help getting reunited with their parents. Most grade-school children walked to school, sometimes as far as a mile from home. Such is no longer the case. Children are being abducted right out of their own beds during the night. Young people are becoming so violent that they are cutting and shooting each other without any remorse or sense of guilt. Some of our children are even murdering their own parents and still expected to receive their inheritance.

With regard to sexual liberties, our society no longer holds a standard of self-restraint. "If it feels good, do it." Our children are becoming sexually active even before they are teenagers. Girls as young as ten years old are becoming pregnant. When they get out on their own, they see no need for marriage; rather they choose to "live together." Relationships are abandoned for the wildest reasons. Those who do marry do not hesitate to cast off the old and go for the new. Remember the conditions described in Noah's time: they were "marrying and giving in marriage." Their thoughts and actions were "only evil continually." We did it all by throwing away sound principles concerning morality in favor of "free speech." Our society has used our own Constitution to throw out the godly principles of a civilized people for the godless liberty of anarchy.

All this has occurred because our society has cast off the influences of our Christian heritage and opened up the floodgates of unholy corruption. As a child in grade school, we daily recited the Pledge of Allegiance. We sang patriotic songs. We had prayer during class. Then there came one atheist who protested that her son was having to be subjected to prayer in school and our nation outlawed prayer in our schools. We caved in to the voice of only one dissenter. These godless apposers of Christ have attacked the words *under God* in our Pledge of Allegiance. They are attempting to remove every religious symbol, from crosses on a hillside to those in our national cemeteries.

Publications like *Playboy* and *Hustler* came out of the poolrooms and into the magazine racks in our markets. In the early days of television, programming was relatively mild. Sexually explicit scenes were not allowed. Vulgarity was not permitted. Movie stars were restrained from having publicized affairs. Children's fare was Howdy Doody, Sesame Street, and Bugs Bunny. Then vulgarity was included, nudity and carnal expression became the norm, and children's programming forsook the Road Runner for Power Rangers and other violent video games. Two generations have fed on sex, drugs, violence, and murder to the extent that our society has been desensitized of all moral restraint, and today we face organized crime, gang wars, drive-by shootings, and deranged young people walking into schools and spraying a hail of bullets into their friends. People are asking, "Why?" The answer is very simple. We kicked God out of our country!

CHAPTER SEVENTEEN

The Rapture

The doctrine of the rapture is confusing and misleading. This doctrine is tied to the return of Christ and the millennial reign with Christ in Jerusalem for one thousand years. See the chapter on the millennium. Basically, this doctrine leads us to believe that Jesus will return to the earth and "rapture" away all the saved and leave the unsaved to suffer through the great "tribulation." Let's look at the scriptures describing these events.

Matthew 24:37-51

"But as the days of Noe were, so shall also the coming of the Son of man be. For as in the days that were before the flood they were eating and drinking, marrying and giving in marriage, until the day that Noe entered into the ark, And knew not until the flood came, and took them all away; so shall also the coming of the Son of man be. Then shall two be in the field; the one shall be taken, and the other left. Two women shall be grinding at the mill; the one shall be taken, and the other left. Watch therefore: for ye know not what hour your Lord doth come. But know this, that if the goodman of the house had known in what watch the thief would come, he would have watched, and would not have suffered his house to be broken up. Therefore be ye also ready: for in such an hour as ye think not the Son of man cometh. Who then is a faithful and wise servant, whom his lord hath made ruler over his household, to give them meat in due season? Blessed is that servant, whom his lord when he cometh shall find so doing. Verily I say unto you, That he shall make him ruler over all his goods. But and if that evil servant shall say in his heart, My lord delayeth his coming; And shall begin to smite his fellowservants, and to eat and drink with the drunken; The lord of that servant shall come in a day when he looketh not for him, and in an hour that he is not aware of, And shall cut him asunder, and appoint him his portion with the hypocrites: there shall be weeping and gnashing of teeth."

You will note in the above scriptures that Jesus is comparing the end of the world with the flood of Noah's time. He talks of the wicked and licentious nature of the world of that day and compares it with the conditions when He is scheduled to appear the second time. The wickedness of men in this generation has truly degenerated into a great depth of sin and corruption. Even those professing salvation are eating and drinking without restraint. People who are faithful and well respected in their church can participate in the revelries of the party on Saturday night, tipping glass for glass with the rest, and be in church on Sunday morning singing "I will follow thee, my Savior" or "I have left all the world to follow Jesus." In the Bible the word drunkenness appears seven times, drunkard five times, drunken thirty-three times, and drunk thirty times. The biblical view of drunkenness is repulsive. This generation has removed for themselves the sting of sin from such practices, giving themselves to revelry without restraint or sense of guilt.

They marry and are given in marriage. I don't think we need to spend a great deal of time on this one. I think we are all aware of the sexual revolution. Many don't even bother getting married at all. They simply cohabit one with another. Some of these common-law relationships last, but most of those people simply travel from one relationship to another. They are all living in sin. More than half of marriages end in divorce, and these couples wind up with each having married more than once, and some a multitude of times. However we look at it, such practice is a promiscuous lifestyle contrary to the Word of God. Jesus and Paul both exposed such practice as sin.

Consider these passages:

> "Thou shalt not commit adultery" (Exodus 20:14).

> "Whosoever putteth away his wife, (divorce) and marrieth another, committeth adultery: and whosoever marrieth her that is put away from her husband committeth adultery" (Luke 16:18).

> "And I say unto you, Whosoever shall put away his wife, except it be for fornication, and shall marry another, committeth adultery: and whoso marrieth her which is put away doth commit adultery" (Matthew 19:9).

To "put away" means to divorce. Both Christ and Paul assert that divorce and remarriage constitutes adultery. Jesus only once grants a small allowance in the case of marital infidelity.

> "For the woman which hath an husband is bound by the law to her husband so long as he liveth; but if the husband be dead, she is loosed from the law of her husband. So then if, while her husband liveth, she be married to another man, she shall be called an adulteress: but if her husband be dead, she is free from that law; so that she is no adulteress, though she be married to another man" (Romans 7:2-3).

Men and women take no heed to the condemnation of the scriptures and move from partner to partner, marrying again and again without a twinge of conscience. This changing of partners is not restricted to the world, but is prominent in most church organizations. Doesn't this all sound about like Jesus' description of Noah's time? And, if Jesus were to come today and bring judgment on them, people would be just as surprised as the community in which Noah lived. Since Jesus made comparison between the events of Noah and the flood with the events of the final judgment, let us consider the conditions.

1. **They were given to revelries.**
   A. Eating and drinking. Living the party life.
   B. At the time of the end, we shall see the same conditions. Our generation has exceeded all others in wickedness. Many of our mainline denominations have compromised their laws, principles, and practices so much that they no longer appear any different from the world. Religious people can curse and swear, spend an evening in the saloon, practice sexual sin and homosexuality, and still be a member in "good standing."

2. **They were marrying and giving in marriage.**
   A. Under the laws of Moses marital promiscuity was rampant. The people of God (Jews) became so brazen in their lust that they devised many ways for a man to discard his wife. If he became unhappy with her for any reason, he could conjure up some excuse for a divorce. When Jesus began to preach on the subject, the Pharisees were astonished:

   > "The Pharisees also came unto him, tempting him,
   > and saying unto him, Is it lawful for a man to put
   > away his wife for every cause?" (Matthew19:3)

   B. Jesus was restoring the plan of God in respect to marriage. God gave only one woman to Adam, and Adam was the only man given to Eve. God said, "Therefore shall a man leave his father and his mother, and shall cleave unto his wife: and they shall be one flesh" (Genesis 2:24). One woman for one man was the plan of God for His creation. Jesus was restoring that plan and let them know that divorce and remarriage created an adulterous condition. Jesus declared that if a man put away his wife, he caused her to commit adultery (Matthew

5:32). The divorced woman upon her remarriage becomes an adulteress, and her divorcing husband is guilty of "causing" her to commit this sin. They are both guilty before God. I wonder how many men and women are members in good standing of some local church who have had two or more marriages. I wonder how many ministers will perform a marriage ceremony for divorced people. Can these defiled people truly expect to enter the ark?

Noah spent 120 years building the ark. During those 120 years, he was a preacher of righteousness. Except for his personal family, no one heeded his preaching, and all the unbelievers were lost, according to these scriptures:

"And spared not the old world, but saved Noah the eighth person, a preacher of righteousness, bringing in the flood upon the world of the ungodly" (2 Peter 2:5).

"Which sometime were disobedient, when once the longsuffering of God waited in the days of Noah, while the ark was a preparing, wherein few, that is, eight souls were saved by water" (1 Peter 3:20).

In our scripture in Matthew 24:40 he continues describing how some will be taken and others left: "Then shall two be in the field; the one shall be taken, and the other left. Two women shall be grinding at the mill; the one shall be taken, and the other left."

Jesus declared that "Many will be called, but few will be chosen." God waited while Noah's ark was being built, but only eight souls were saved. God is now waiting while the church is being built, and only those who are truly inside the church that Jesus built will be saved. Jesus did not build the multiplicity of denominations; they are man-made organizations and as such are not the Church of God. Being a member in good standing in one of those organizations will not suffice. Those organizations are not included in the Church of God (see the chapter

"The Church"). Therefore, the ark of safety or the church will contain only those few obedient believers who surrender to the Lord Jesus Christ and are obedient to His Word, living according the godly and holy principles contained in the Bible.

> "Nevertheless when the Son of man cometh, shall he find faith on the earth?" (Luke 18:8)

> "And except those days should be shortened, there should no flesh be saved: but for the elect's sake those days shall be shortened" (Matthew 24:22).

These texts clearly show that when Jesus returns again, that faith will be so weak that He will have to shorten the days to final judgment or else there will be no one left to come back for.

The Bible also makes it clear that Jesus will return for His church. It is called His Second Coming.

> "Which also said, Ye men of Galilee, why stand ye gazing up into heaven? this same Jesus, which is taken up from you into heaven, shall so come in like manner as ye have seen him go into heaven" (Acts 1:11).

> "And if I go and prepare a place for you, I will come again, and receive you unto myself; that where I am, there ye may be also" (John 14:3).

The initial scripture for this chapter says that one shall be taken and the other left; that is simply telling us that when the Lord returns, He will claim those who are ready, and the rest will be left or rejected or "cast out." Notice the next part of the scripture.

"Watch therefore: for ye know not what hour your Lord doth come. But know this, that if the goodman of the house had known in what watch the thief would come, he would have watched, and would not have suffered his house to be broken up. Therefore be ye also ready: for in such an hour as ye think not the Son of man cometh."

Many scriptures tell of the coming of the Lord. The story of the ten virgins in Matthew 25 tells of five wise and five foolish virgins. The wise kept their soul ablaze with the oil of the Spirit of God. The foolish had allowed their lamps to burn out. The Lord came; they were not ready and were cast out. There is no indication that Jesus made provision to pick them up later after some period of tribulation or during some millennium.

The following scriptures speak on one primary theme, "the last day." Any logical mind knows that when the last has come, there is nothing more.

> "And this is the Father's will which hath sent me, that of all which he hath given me I should lose nothing, but should raise it up again at the last day. And this is the will of him that sent me, that every one which seeth the Son, and believeth on him, may have everlasting life: and I will raise him up at the last day" (John 6:39-40).

> "No man can come to me, except the Father which hath sent me draw him: and I will raise him up at the last day" (John 6:44).

> "Whoso eateth my flesh, and drinketh my blood, hath eternal life; and I will raise him up at the last day" (John 6:54).

> "Martha saith unto him, I know that he shall rise again in the resurrection at the last day" (John 11:24).

> "He that rejecteth me, and receiveth not my words, hath one that judgeth him: the word that I have spoken, the same shall judge him in the last day" (John 12:48).

The first four texts talk of the Lord coming for His faithful at the last day. The fifth text talks of the judgment that will occur at the last day. Both the righteous and the unrighteous are subject to resurrection. The righteous will be raised to the resurrection of life, the unrighteous to the resurrection of damnation.

> "And have hope toward God, which they themselves also allow, that there shall be a resurrection of the dead, both of the just and unjust" (Acts 24:15).

> "Marvel not at this: for the hour is coming, in the which all that are in the graves shall hear his voice, And shall come forth; they that have done good, unto the resurrection of life; and they that have done evil, unto the resurrection of damnation" (John 5:28-29).

The most compelling scripture on the subject of the resurrection is 1 Thessalonians 4:14-17: "For if we believe that Jesus died and rose again, even so them also which sleep in Jesus will God bring with him. For this we say unto you by the word of the Lord, that we which are alive and remain unto the coming of the Lord shall not prevent them which are asleep. For the Lord himself shall descend from heaven with a shout, with the voice of the archangel, and with the trump of God: and the dead in Christ shall rise first: Then we which are alive and remain shall be caught up together with them in the clouds, to meet the Lord in the air: and so shall we ever be with the Lord."

This scripture is used to prove the rapture. But consider what it says. First it tells us that when the last day comes, Jesus, with all the saints who have gone on before, will come with a shout and the blowing of the trumpets and we who are alive in body at that time will not go before those in the graves. The graves will deliver up their dead first and we who are alive will be joined by them. Gravity will release its hold and we, together with them, will be caught up together to meet Jesus in the air. The scripture says, "so shall we ever be with the Lord." There is no indication of anything beyond that event. Note also that all these events occur at the *last day*. If the church is to return at some future time, then these verses are inaccurate, because it says that "so shall we *ever* be with the Lord." The meeting between Jesus and His saints will be "in the air," or heaven, not on the earth in some millennial reign. At the *last day*.

The word *rapture* does not appear anywhere in the Bible, in neither the Old nor the New Testament. It is a created doctrine to establish one or more possible outcomes. One is to establish that Jesus is coming to earth again to set up a kingdom at Jerusalem. Jesus Himself put that one to rest by telling us that the kingdom was not an earthly kingdom but a spiritual one.

> "And when he was demanded of the Pharisees, when the kingdom of God should come, he answered them and said, The kingdom of God cometh not with observation: Neither shall they say, Lo here! or, lo there! for, behold, the kingdom of God is within you" (Luke 17:20-21).

Another purpose is to establish more than one coming to allow another opportunity to make the sinners life right after a period of suffering in the tribulation. However, because the scripture says that Jesus will return at the last day, there is neither time nor allowance for another event. The last day is the last day, and there is no place or time for a kingdom in Jerusalem. For those who choose to believe that Jesus would reestablish the Jews, remember that Jesus Himself pronounced judgment on Jerusalem while He was preparing to leave this earth. Jesus had preached to them, they had rejected Him, and Jesus sadly declared Jerusalem desolate and deserted. See for instance, this passage from Matthew:

> "O Jerusalem, Jerusalem, thou that killest the prophets, and stonest them which are sent unto thee, how often would I have gathered thy children together, even as a hen gathereth her chickens under her wings, and ye would not! Behold, your house is left unto you desolate. For I

> say unto you, Ye shall not see me henceforth, till ye shall
> say, Blessed is he that cometh in the name of the Lord"
> (Matthew 23:37-39).

The Jews had rejected Jesus, and after many centuries of effort He is finally leaving them for true believers of any nation. Remember how when Moses erected the tabernacle in the wilderness, it was only a tent until the glory of God entered the holy chamber? At that entering, the glory of God was so bright that the people could not look upon it or enter into it. Likewise, the temple of Solomon was filled with the glory of God, and the same spiritual conditions were applied. This all means that as long as God is resident in the tabernacle or temple, the people remain God's people. When that spirit departs the temple, it is no longer a safe haven for the soul. Paul makes it clear in this passage from Romans that those who were born to the nation of Israel were no longer such in the eyes of God:

> "Not as though the word of God hath taken none effect.
> For they are not all Israel, which are of Israel: Neither,
> because they are the seed of Abraham, are they all children:
> but, In Isaac shall thy seed be called" (Romans 9:6-7).

Abraham had children by Sarah, Hagar, and Keturah. But God established that the kingdom would be vested in the children of faith. Isaac. Paul is bringing this message more clearly, declaring that it is no longer the Jews who are the children of God, but the children of faith, whether Jew or Gentile. The kingdom of God is not a literal kingdom upon this earth but a spiritual kingdom within the heart. And lastly, this world and all its wickedness will be done away with, not purged.

Second Peter 3:10-12 says, "But the day of the Lord will come as a thief in the night; in the which the heavens shall pass away with a great noise, and the elements shall melt with fervent heat, the earth also and the works that are therein shall be burned up. Seeing then that all these things shall be dissolved, what manner of persons ought ye to be in all holy conversation and godliness, Looking for and hasting unto the coming of the day of God, wherein the heavens being on fire shall be dissolved, and the elements shall melt with fervent heat?"

Who would want to remain on this world? All of the scriptures pertaining to the second coming of Christ reference the singular tense. The last day, the judgment, or the coming of the Lord is always referred to as a single coming event. Not a single scripture uses the plural, "second comings, next to the last day or second judgment." What can be beyond the last of anything?

Satan is reaping a great harvest of souls in those seeking to find some "loophole" in the Word of God. People who desire to live a worldly life contrary to the Word of God need to find some scripture or doctrine that will make allowances for their sinful lives. The rapture is as good as any. With such a doctrine, Satan has offered unholy men an avenue of redemption or hope of eternal life after suffering a tribulation. I challenge any sound thinker to find any inkling of such allowances in the Bible. We are commanded, not requested, to be holy. We are commanded, not requested, to live sinless lives. We are commanded to turn from the world and be not a partaker of its evil deeds. In the days of Noah when God said, "Enter the ark," the fate of the populace was sealed. There was neither rapture nor reprieve. God shut the door, and when God shuts the door, the door is closed. When the rains came, plead as they might, Noah could not and God would not open the door. The door was shut.

When Jesus comes to gather His remnant church, He will appear in the air. He will be accompanied by the "heavenly host." The trumpet will blow and the judgment will commence. The righteous will be invited to "ever be with the Lord." The unrighteous will be cast into the lake of fire.

Revelation 20:15 says, "And whosoever was not found written in the book of life was cast into the lake of fire."

John 5:28-29 says, "Marvel not at this: for the hour is coming, in the which all that are in the graves shall hear his voice, And shall come forth; they that have done good, unto the resurrection of life; and they that have done evil, unto the resurrection of damnation."

And that is how the Bible describes the end.

CHAPTER EIGHTEEN

Strong Drink

Beer is not mentioned in the Bible. Wine and strong drink are mentioned many times. Wine and strong drink were not refused the normal Israelite. However, wine and strong drink were denied the priests, kings, and princes, because they impair the judgment of those to whom others look for guidance.

Strong drink describes any beverage that intoxicates. Priests were forbidden strong drink when officiating at the altar of sacrifice. Nazarites were not to indulge in strong drink during the time of their vow. Kings and princes were also limited in the use of strong drink. Strong drink was not refused the general Israelite, but much admonition was given to avoid its intoxicating results. Those who drank to excess were identified as "drunkards." Consider the following scriptures:

> "But they also have erred through wine, and through strong drink are out of the way; the priest and the prophet have erred through strong drink, they are swallowed up of wine, they are out of the way through strong drink; they err in vision, they stumble in judgment" (Isaiah 28:7).

> "Wine is a mocker, strong drink is raging: and whosoever is deceived thereby is not wise" (Proverbs 20:1).

"Who hath woe? Who hath sorrow? Who hath contentions? Who hath babbling? Who hath wounds without cause? Who hath redness of eyes? They that tarry long at the wine; they that go to seek mixed wine. Look not thou upon the wine when it is red, when it giveth his colour in the cup, when it moveth itself aright" (Proverbs 23:29-31).

The idea that beer is not "strong drink" is no defense for using it. The definition above identifies any "intoxicating" beverage as strong drink. Beer intoxicates and thus fits the Bible definition for "strong drink." Strong drink was forbidden the kings, princes, and priests when officiating at the temple. In the Christian dispensation, by entering the kingdom through the "new birth," we become children of God. God is the supreme king, and as His children we are princes of the King. He has also elevated the Christian to the position of "kings and priests" and as such Christians are not permitted indulgence in intoxicating beverages.

Revelation 5:10 says, "And hast made us unto our God kings and priests: and we shall reign on the earth."

And Proverbs 31:4, "It is not for kings, O Lemuel, it is not for kings to drink wine; nor for princes strong drink."

The Christian is also part of the residency of the Holy Spirit since the Holy Spirit takes up residency in His true temple, the hearts of the people of God. We call it sanctification, the infilling of the Holy Ghost or the habitation of God: "In whom ye also are builded together for an habitation of God through the Spirit" (Ephesians 2:22).

God uses the hearts of His people for a habitation. He will not inhabit a polluted temple. If a Holy God is going to inhabit a temple, that temple must also be holy. God will not occupy a drunken heart.

"What? know ye not that your body is the temple of the Holy Ghost which is in you, which ye have of God, and ye are not your own?" (1 Corinthians 6:19).

If we are going to pollute the temple of God, which is the body, by filling it with alcohol, drugs, tobacco, and other pollutants, we can expect God to respond: "If any man defile the temple of God, him shall God destroy; for the temple of God is holy, which temple ye are" (1 Corinthians 3:17).

First Thessalonians 5:22 says, "Abstain from all appearance of evil."

How can we justify allowing any product that can potentially harm the body to enter the body?

In modern times we try to ease our guilt and responsibility by renaming a condition from one of revulsion to one of pity and tolerance. The Bible's definition of an abuser of strong drink is "drunkard." Modern society chooses to name it "alcoholism." Many people today are trying to identify alcoholism as a disease. By making it a disease we relieve ourselves of responsibility and seek pity and tolerance. I pose one question to those wishing to make alcoholism a disease: What germ or virus invaded the body to cause one to become an alcoholic? My friend, alcoholism is not a disease; it is a condition we bring on ourselves by indulging in strong drink.

Is this or is this not a fact: a person who never takes a drink of intoxicants will never become an alcoholic.

Who then is responsible for the alcoholic? The alcoholic is responsible for himself. There is no germ or virus or mutant cell or gene that "causes" alcoholism. We do it by conscious choice.

Alcoholism destroys the body. Many die of various maladies each year from the effects of alcoholism. God's judgment rests on the alcoholic rather than His sympathy, because by indulging in strong drink we pollute the body with body-killing substances. The Bible says that whosoever defiles the body will face the wrath of God. Since the body is the temple of the Holy Ghost, we invite God's judgment when we introduce liquor and drugs into the body.

1 Corinthians 3:17 says, "If any man defile the temple of God, him shall God destroy; for the temple of God is holy, which temple ye are."

CHAPTER NINETEEN

The Gift of Tongues

As with many other doctrines there is much misapplication of the Bible's use of tongues. Of all the doctrines misapplied, Satan has taken this very simple and useful gift way out of proportion. The human need for something new and exciting or a new revelation allows Satan to distort the truth into gross error. Such is the case with the gift of tongues.

In my early childhood, I attended a Pentecostal church for about a year. Speaking in tongues was a prominent feature of the regular worship service, along with other demonstrations. Various ones would fall under the power and give utterances; some would have some physical demonstration not under their own control. One young woman, the pastor's daughter, would back up against a wall and bounce off it as though hands had taken her by the shoulders and were slamming her against it repeatedly. All the while this physical activity was taking place, she was stammering some unintelligible utterances. In those days, people who experienced this were known as holy rollers. It was not unusual for someone to be "slain in the spirit" and fall to the floor and roll around uncontrollably. Sometimes women falling under this spirit would be compromised as their dresses failed to keep them covered, which is a violation of the command for women to be modest in dress. This in itself is evidence that something is wrong, as the Holy Spirit would never cause one to violate the Word of God. Oh, Satan is a crafty one.

As we begin to look at the scriptures for a revealing of the truth on the subject of tongues, let us go to the first occurrence of the phenomenon. In the early days of Bible history we find that Nimrod, the great-grandson of Noah, moved the people to build a tower high enough to reach heaven (Genesis 11:1-8). In order to put a stop to this folly of the people and to disperse the people into the world, God confounded their language into a multitude of languages. Those who understood one another colonized together and separated themselves from those they could not understand. Thus, the people were dispersed throughout the world. The city, because of the babbling of confused languages, became known as Babylon.

In the New Testament we have an occurrence on the day of Pentecost, where the disciples, as they were empowered by the Holy Spirit, began to speak in other tongues. Before ascending into heaven, Jesus told His disciples that they would speak with new tongues: "And these signs shall follow them that believe; In my name shall they cast out devils; they shall speak with new tongues" (Mark 16:17)

At Pentecost, they who were in the upper chamber began to speak in languages other than their native language, "other tongues," as told in Acts 2:4: "And they were all filled with the Holy Ghost, and began to speak with other tongues, as the Spirit gave them utterance."

Now pay close attention to the following scripture, which tells us exactly what true Bible tongues are: "Now when this was noised abroad, the multitude came together, and were confounded, because that every man heard them speak in his own language. And they were all amazed and marvelled, saying one to another, Behold, are not all these which speak Galilaeans? And how hear we every man in our own tongue, wherein we were born? Parthians, and Medes, and Elamites, and the dwellers in Mesopotamia, and in Judaea, and Cappadocia, in Pontus, and Asia, Phrygia, and Pamphylia, in Egypt, and in the parts of Libya about Cyrene, and strangers of Rome, Jews and proselytes, Cretes and Arabians, we do hear them speak in our tongues the wonderful works of God. And they were all amazed, and were in doubt, saying one to another, What meaneth this?" (Acts 2:6-12).

As these disciples spoke in "other" tongues or languages, pay attention to who was listening. The multitude was astonished because they each heard these disciples speaking in "their own languages." These Parthians, Medes, and other foreign visitors did not hear the disciples speaking in some "heavenly" language, they heard them speaking in their own native tongue. The above scripture alone should be enough for any honest heart to understand that true Bible tongues are not some unintelligible utterance but the God-given gift of speaking in another "known" language. The biblical account of the utterances at Pentecost in no way suggests anything other than "known" languages.

For those who hold that the baptism of the Holy Ghost is evidenced by speaking in tongues, why is it then that so many people who were filled did not speak in unknown tongues? There is no mention in the Bible that Jesus ever spoke in an unknown tongue. John the Baptist was filled with the Holy Ghost from the womb, and yet there is no mention of his speaking in any foreign tongue. In the following scripture we see where the Holy Spirit was manifested and yet there was no speaking in unknown tongues.

> "Now when the apostles which were at Jerusalem heard that Samaria had received the word of God, they sent unto them Peter and John: Who, when they were come down, prayed for them, that they might receive the Holy Ghost: (For as yet he was fallen upon none of them: only they were baptized in the name of the Lord Jesus.) Then laid they their hands on them, and they received the Holy Ghost" (Acts 8:14-17).

Error concerning the gift of tongues began early on, and Paul deals very intensely with the subject in Chapter 14 of First Corinthians. Paul begins right off with the mention of the gift of tongues. In verse 1 Paul advises us to seek spiritual gifts, but emphasizes the ability to prophesy.

In verse 5 Paul puts greater value on prophesying than on the gift of tongues. As a matter of fact, prophesying has greater value to Paul than all the spiritual gifts.

"Follow after charity, and desire spiritual gifts, but rather that ye may prophesy" (1 Corinthians 14:1).

"I would that ye all spake with tongues, *but rather* that ye prophesied: for greater is he that prophesieth than he that speaketh with tongues, except he interpret, that the church may receive edifying" (1 Corinthians 14:5).

How could Paul take preference over the gift of tongues if it were the evidence of the infilling of the Holy Ghost, which is commanded of all believers? Paul prefers prophesying or declaring the Word of the Lord to speaking in tongues. If we assign an order of importance based on the order in which the gifts are mentioned, the gift of tongues would be the least of the gifts. In this fourteenth chapter of First Corinthians Paul deals with the subject of the gift of tongues very deeply. We are here going to follow Paul's reasoning through this chapter.

"For he that speaketh in an unknown tongue speaketh not unto men, but unto God: for no man understandeth him; howbeit in the spirit he speaketh mysteries. But he that prophesieth speaketh unto men to edification, and exhortation, and comfort" (1 Corinthians 14:2-3).

The modern tongues doctrine holds that the term *unknown* in this verse represents a spiritual language known only to the Holy Spirit and that the Holy Spirit is using the mouth of the speaker to speak of heavenly things. These heavenly utterances are not understood by any human being; they are the language of the Spirit. We will speak of "interpretation" later. Paul again in this verse sets preference of prophesying over tongues for the purpose of edification of the church. Whatever we do, whether praying, prophesying, or exhorting, such is to be for the edification of the church. Orating in an unintelligible language does not edify anyone.

> "He that speaketh in an unknown tongue edifieth himself; but he that prophesieth edifieth the church" (1 Corinthians 14:4).

Here we see that the man who is speaking in an "unknown" tongue edifies himself. If the man himself does not know what he is speaking, he cannot be edified. By such reasoning we see that the term *unknown* does not refer to the man doing the speaking, but to those listening to his speech.

> "I would that ye all spake with tongues, but rather that ye prophesied: for greater is he that prophesieth than he that speaketh with tongues, except he interpret, that the church may receive edifying" (First Corinthians 14:5).

In this verse, Paul plainly makes tongues an inferior gift to that of edifying the body of Christ. Again Paul hints that there is an interpretation expected of those speaking in an unknown tongue. Paul says, "I would that ye all spake with tongues." Remember the vast host of different cultures abiding in Jerusalem at Pentecost? Being able to communicate across the various language barriers would be very helpful.

> "Now, brethren, if I come unto you speaking with tongues, what shall I profit you, except I shall speak to you either by revelation, or by knowledge, or by prophesying, or by doctrine? And even things without life giving sound, whether pipe or harp, except they give a distinction in the sounds, how shall it be known what is piped or harped? For if the trumpet give an uncertain sound, who shall prepare himself to the battle?" (1 Corinthians 14:6-9)

Here Paul reasons that there is no profit to the congregation from one speaking in an unknown tongue unless he is able to translate his words into some that can be understood by his hearers. Paul continues his reasoning with the illustration of the pipe, harp, or trumpet. These instruments are used for alerting the hearers for an event. For those who have been in the military, you will recall the bugle piping reveille, mess call, attention to colors, taps, and so on. If the bugler did not know the melody for mess call, who would know it was time to eat? If the cavalry bugler sounded "Mary Had a Little Lamb" instead of "Charge!" the battle would be lost. Paul uses the same reasoning for the words we speak. "So likewise ye, except ye utter by the tongue words easy to be understood, how shall it be known what is spoken? for ye shall speak into the air."

> "There are, it may be, so many kinds of voices in the world, and none of them is without signification. Therefore if I know not the meaning of the voice, I shall be unto him that speaketh a barbarian, and he that speaketh shall be a barbarian unto me. Even so ye, forasmuch as ye are zealous of spiritual gifts, seek that ye may excel to the edifying of the church" (1 Corinthians 14:10-12).

Paul tells us that there is no voice (language) in this world that is without signification. This statement gives us to understand that every word that is uttered is understandable to someone. These voices are languages known in the world such as Hebrew, English, Spanish, and so on. For those speaking English, Spanish is an unknown language. To him who speaks Hebrew, English is an unknown language. However, whatever language we speak, the language is not unknown to the one speaking. Again, Paul makes it clear that our purpose is the edification or encouragement of the church.

> "Wherefore let him that speaketh in an unknown tongue pray that he may interpret. For if I pray in an unknown tongue, my spirit prayeth, but my understanding is unfruitful. What is it then? I will pray with the spirit, and I will pray with the understanding also: I will sing with

the spirit, and I will sing with the understanding also" (1 Corinthians 14:13-15).

In the above verse, Paul indicates that his "understanding is unfruitful." Advocates of the tongues doctrine will use this as proof that there is a language unknown to the speaker. Look closer at the whole verse. Paul tells us to pray that we may be able to interpret if we use an unknown language. If this unknown language is unknown to me, there is nothing I can do to gain understanding and the balance of this verse makes no sense. "What is it then? I will pray with the spirit, and I will pray with the understanding also: I will sing with the spirit, and I will sing with the understanding also." If I have no understanding of the language I speak, then it is impossible for me to comply with Paul's commandment to "pray and sing" with "understanding also."

> "Else when thou shalt bless with the spirit, how shall he that occupieth the room of the unlearned say Amen at thy giving of thanks, seeing he understandeth not what thou sayest? For thou verily givest thanks well, but the other is not edified" (1 Corinthians 14:16-17).

Paul reasons that when we speak in a language different from that which others in the room speak, they will not be able to be in agreement with our prayer or speech. Paul says, "For thou verily givest thanks well, but the other is not edified." How would Paul know he was giving thanks if he knew not what he was saying? It should be coming clear that the modern doctrine of a tongue that is unknown to the speaker is not what Paul was teaching.

> "I thank my God, I speak with tongues more than ye all: Yet in the church I had rather speak five words with my understanding, that by my voice I might teach others also, than ten thousand words in an unknown tongue" (1 Corinthians 14:18-19).

Look at Paul's attitude with respect to tongues. "I thank my God, I speak with tongues more than ye all." Paul definitely had the gift of tongues in abundance. Don't forget the tongues at Pentecost. The city was filled with travelers from many nations who heard the disciples speak in the tongues or languages in which they were born. Paul in his travels could be surrounded by one language or dialect today and by another in another area tomorrow. Being able to communicate with the locals was necessary, and we all know it would be impossible for him to learn all the different languages of the people where he traveled. Therefore, God gave him the gift of speaking to other cultures and be understood by them. Let me share an illustration from modern times. A Norwegian minister of the Church of God early in the twentieth century was asked to preach to a German-speaking congregation. This minister spoke Norwegian and English. He protested and declined several times, but at the insistence of the pastor, finally agreed to preach to the German congregation. He said, however, that he would have to preach in his own language. The minister preached in his native language and was understood in perfect German. This is the true gift of tongues, the ability by the gift of God to speak and be understood by those who speak another language.

> "In the law it is written, With men of other tongues and other lips will I speak unto this people; and yet for all that will they not hear me, saith the Lord. Wherefore tongues are for a sign, not to them that believe, but to them that believe not: but prophesying serveth not for them that believe not, but for them which believe. If therefore the whole church be come together into one place, and all speak with tongues, and there come in those that are unlearned, or unbelievers, will they not say that ye are mad? But if all prophesy, and there come in one that believeth not, or one unlearned, he is convinced of all, he is judged of all: And thus are the secrets of his heart made manifest; and so falling down on his face he will worship God, and report that God is in you of a truth." (1 Corinthians 14:21-25)

Early in my Christian life I was in debate with a small group of Pentecostal people who were trying to prove to me that speaking in tongues was the evidence of the infilling of the Holy Ghost. I asked, "Is speaking in tongues a sign to me as a believer that I have been filled with the Holy Ghost?" The answer was yes. I then referred them to the above verse and asked, "How then do you deal with 1 Corinthians 14:22, "Wherefore tongues are for a sign, not to them that believe, but to them that believe not?" Tongues are not a sign to the believer or anyone else proving the infilling of the Holy Ghost. Also, we said early in this chapter that there were many in the apostolic times who were filled with the Holy Ghost and yet there was no mention of their speaking in tongues. Paul has made it clear in this chapter that tongues are an inferior gift subordinate to preaching and edification of the assembly. If an unbeliever comes into an assembly speaking in a variety of unintelligible utterances, he will ridicule that congregation. However, if he comes into an assembly preaching, praying, and testifying intelligently, all will be convinced of the truth: "And thus are the secrets of his heart made manifest; and so falling down on his face he will worship God, and report that God is in you of a truth" (1 Corinthians 14:25)

> "How is it then, brethren? when ye come together, everyone
> of you hath a psalm, hath a doctrine, hath a tongue, hath
> a revelation, hath an interpretation. Let all things be done
> unto edifying" (1 Corinthians 14:26).

In the preceding verse Paul is simply reiterating that whatever we do in the service is to lead to edifying and not to confusion.

> "If any man speak in an unknown tongue, let it be by
> two, or at the most by three, and that by course; and let
> one interpret. But if there be no interpreter, let him keep
> silence in the church; and let him speak to himself, and to
> God" (1 Corinthians 14:27-28).

Here again is where modern tongues teachers violate the Word of God. If one speaks in an unknown tongue and there is no one to interpret, he is commanded to keep silence in the church. Having some experience in the Pentecostal movement in my youth, I have seen this verse ignored. As time has progressed, there has been a complete abandonment of the scriptural conditions for speaking in an unknown tongue. The Pentecostal doctrine of tongues has always been believed to be an utterance by the Spirit through the mouth of the believer. However, it was acknowledged that an interpreter was necessary if one was to speak in tongues. I observed a man one time who stood up to testify, orated in an unintelligible speech, and then sat down. This man had just disobeyed the Word of God. He had no idea if there would be an interpreter, and he is the one commanded to keep silence in the absence of an interpreter. Across the congregation another man stood up and gave an interpretation. This process is not in harmony with the Word of God, because the first speaker is to keep silence *until* an interpreter is available, and this man had no idea if an interpreter would stand up.

Satan is a master of counterfeit doctrine and will take honest and sincere people and inch them along the path to scriptural disobedience. At least in the example above, there was some attempt to comply with the requirement of an interpreter. Now let's see where the doctrine has gone today. Watch modern Pentecostal evangelists preaching today. Some will be preaching and periodically give an expression in tongues. They will rock back and forth, speaking in tongues and in their language. No longer is there any attempt to have an interpretation, which is a clear violation of scriptural requirement for those speaking in another language. The Holy Spirit will never lead anyone to violate any part of the Word of God, and any spirit that does so is not the Spirit of God. Such has simply become accepted as a spiritual manifestation, and the Word of God is ignored. Some fall under the spirit of tongues when converted, when prayed for, and at other times without any sign of an interpreter, without any explanation. Why is there not an interpreter?

First Corinthians 14:29-33 says, "Let the prophets speak two or three, and let the other judge. If any thing be revealed to another that sitteth by, let the first hold his peace. For ye may all prophesy one by one, that all may learn, and all may be comforted. And the spirits of the prophets are subject to the prophets. For God is not the author of confusion, but of peace, as in all churches of the saints."

The prophets in this context are preachers, exhorters, testifiers, and so on. There may be a number of people with a message, a testimony, or an exhortation. It is perfectly acceptable for all of them to express themselves but not in a disruptive manner. One by one they are permitted to speak for the "edification" of the church. Paul in verse 32 throws a real curveball to the advocators of the doctrine that tongues are an involuntary manifestation of the spirit. Paul says that "the spirits of the prophets are subject to the prophets." Therefore, the spirit is subject to the control of the believer, and any spirit that takes control of one's faculties, or that overpowers one's own conscious control, causing one to fall to the floor, swoon, or do any involuntary acts, is not the Spirit of God. Such a spirit is forcing the believer to violate the Word of God, and that is not the Spirit of God. It is another spirit that has taken control of the believer. The Holy Spirit will never lead one to violate God's Word. The apostle concludes these verses by reminding us that "God is not the author of confusion, but of peace, as in all churches of the saints."

> "If any man think himself to be a prophet, or spiritual, let him acknowledge that the things that I write unto you are the commandments of the Lord. But if any man be ignorant, let him be ignorant. Wherefore, brethren, covet to prophesy, and forbid not to speak with tongues. Let all things be done decently and in order" (1 Corinthians 14:37-15:1).

Here Paul reminds us that the things contained in this message are the commandments of God. But, he also recognizes that many need some special manifestation in order to feel spiritual. God's Word never promised some manifestation as evidence of His approval on one's life. "The just shall live by his faith." God does bless His people and does manifest Himself in many ways, but such manifestation is for the edification and encouragement of the believer and to the glory of the Father. For those who insist on following a doctrine that perverts the Word of God, Paul says, "let him be ignorant"

CONCLUSION

In the foregoing chapters we have examined many of the common beliefs among the various Christian denominations. The fact that there are varying interpretations and beliefs is not surprising. Understanding the Bible is not learned in schools and colleges. The proper application of the Bible is learned while sitting at the feet of Jesus.

I do not mean to imply that the classroom has no value. We do have many highly qualified pastors, instructors, and counselors who can expound on the Word of God with great competence. But those instructors and counselors cannot impart the spiritual knowledge that can save the soul. The saving grace of the Lord Jesus Christ comes by "revelation" from God. The duty of our counselors and pastors is to lead the seeker to Jesus through prayer and the study of the Word of God. And the Holy Spirit is the revealer of truth.

The reason that there are so many different interpretations of the Bible is that men are attempting to decipher the Word of God intellectually, and that is not possible. Man's intellect cannot possibly comprehend the mind of God. Consequently many are left with a scriptural analysis based on human reasoning and trying to figure out "what makes sense." There is only one source of truth in interpreting the Word of God, and that is God Himself through the Holy Spirit.

James 1:5 says, "If any of you lack wisdom, let him ask of God, that giveth to all men liberally, and upbraideth not; and it shall be given him."

It has not been my intention to criticize anyone's beliefs. Rather, I want to challenge the reader to seek the truth of God's Word by looking to God directly in prayer, asking Him to reveal His Word. The wisdom of man will fail every time.

John 16:13 says, "Howbeit when he, the Spirit of truth, is come, he will guide you into all truth: for he shall not speak of himself; but whatsoever he shall hear, that shall he speak: and he will shew you things to come."

The apostle Paul described the early church as people who did not believe the preacher simply because they loved the preacher. They wanted the truth, and they went to the source of truth, the Hebrew scriptures. If people today would follow that practice and search the scriptures to see if their preacher is telling them the truth, there would be much less confusion in our religious world. Note what Paul says here.

> "They received the word with all readiness of mind, and searched the scriptures daily, whether those things were so" (Acts 17:11).

It is with a great sense of love for the truth of God's Word and the enlightenment of honest hearts that I present these pages. May God bless them to the edification of the body of our Lord and Savior Jesus Christ. Amen.

William L. Laughlin